W9-BOM-544

love at first bark

love at first bark

HOW SAVING A DOG
CAN SOMETIMES HELP YOU
SAVE YOURSELF

Julie Klam

RIVERHEAD BOOKS

a member of Penguin Group (USA) Inc.

New York

2011

RIVERHEAD BOOKS
Published by the Penguin Group
Penguin Group (USA) Inc., 375 Hudson Street,
New York, New York 10014, USA • Penguin Group (Canada),
90 Eglinton Avenue East, Suite 700, Toronto, Ontario M4P 2Y3,
Canada (a division of Pearson Penguin Canada Inc.) • Penguin Books Ltd,
80 Strand, London WC2R 0RL, England • Penguin Ireland, 25 St Stephen's Green,
Dublin 2, Ireland (a division of Penguin Books Ltd) • Penguin Group (Australia),
250 Camberwell Road, Camberwell, Victoria 3124, Australia (a division of Pearson
Australia Group Pty Ltd) • Penguin Books India Pvt Ltd, 11 Community Centre,
Panchsheel Park, New Delhi–110 017, India • Penguin Group (NZ), 67 Apollo
Drive, Rosedale, North Shore 0632, New Zealand (a division of Pearson
New Zealand Ltd) • Penguin Books (South Africa) (Pty) Ltd,
24 Sturdee Avenue, Rosebank, Johannesburg 2196,
South Africa

Penguin Books Ltd, Registered Offices:
80 Strand, London WC2R 0RL, England

Library of Congress Cataloging-in-Publication Data

Klam, Julie.
Love at first bark: how saving a dog can sometimes help you save yourself / Julie Klam.
p.   cm.
ISBN 978-1-59448-828-3
1. Klam, Julie.   2. Dog rescue—Anecdotes.   3. Dogs—Therapeutic use.   4. Dog owners—
Biography.   5. Human-animal relationships.   I. Title.
RM931.D63K5.   2011   2011030053
615.8'5158—dc23

Printed in the United States of America
1   3   5   7   9   10   8   6   4   2

BOOK DESIGN BY AMANDA DEWEY

Some names and identifying characteristics have been changed
to protect the privacy of the individuals involved.

While the author has made every effort to provide accurate telephone numbers and Internet addresses
at the time of publication, neither the publisher nor the author assumes any responsibility for errors,
or for changes that occur after publication. Further, the publisher does not have any control over and
does not assume any responsibility for author or third-party websites or their content.

*Penguin is committed to publishing works of quality and integrity.
In that spirit, we are proud to offer this book to our readers;
however, the story, the experiences, and the words
are the author's alone.*

For my father

We mock the thing we are to be.

Mel Brooks, as the 2,000-Year-Old Man

Contents

Mercy to animals means mercy to mankind.

HENRY BERGH, founder of the American Society
for the Prevention of Cruelty to Animals

What Shih Tzus need rescuing anyway?
You don't see Shih Tzus straggling around the streets
in an old coat, "Help, alms for the poor."

SCOTT DONLAN, *Best in Show*

love at first bark

Morris the Pit Bull, Couples Therapist

It was six forty-five a.m., and I was heading back to my apartment with my three dogs, Wisteria, Fiorello, and Beatrice. The street lamps still glowed, but the neighborhood was not awake. The emptiness made it that much easier to spot the nine men in navy jackets, walking around the front of my building, looking up at the windows and talking to each other, with guns hanging out of their pockets. They saw me and smiled uneasily and followed me up the stairs. I noticed that all of these men—tall or short—were huge, built like either safes or refrigerators, but they looked at me a little warily. I'm smallish and I was walking three sub-twenty-pound dogs with adorably patterned harnesses and leashes.

"Good morning," said the guy who appeared to be the captain.

"Do you want to come in?" I asked.

"Yes." He looked down at my dogs. "Do they bite?"

"No," I replied, and they all relaxed. Over their sweaters, they sported giant bulletproof vests, and their pants were tucked into thick black leather boots. What exactly were they afraid my terriers would do to them? Fray their shoelaces?

As I unlocked the door, the captain remarked, "Good thing you came along, the super isn't answering his bell." This is the minor problem with the security in my building. The criminals live here, and the cops can't seem to gain entrance.

"He's probably asleep," I said, opening the lock and holding the door, my three dogs behind me.

"Have you lived here awhile?"

"A little over a year."

"Are you social? Do you know a lot of people in the building?"

"Not a lot," I answered.

He showed me a picture of a young Latino male, which was blurry since it had been taken by a closed-circuit camera. I had no idea who he was, but apparently this was his last known residence.

"Sorry," I said, really wishing I could help, like in an old movie: "Hey, sure, I know dat guy, Ralphie Beans, from da tent flaw!" But alas, I did not. The elevator opened and half the cops got in. The others looked at my dogs and said they'd take the stairs . . . to the tenth floor. I had to laugh a little. I went into my apartment and double-bolted the doors and woke up my daughter, Violet, for school.

In the summer of 2009, I was living with my husband, daughter, and then four dogs on 106th Street and Broadway. It was a lovely two-bedroom, one-bathroom apartment in a prewar doorman building with a Duane Reade pharmacy within skipping distance and numerous other conveniences (hardware stores, restaurants, bagel shops) abounding nearby. We were going on five relatively happy years there. The problem was that the rent kept going up despite our income's refusal to do the same. We decided to look for a cheaper place. Since our daughter was firmly planted in one of the area's better public schools, we needed to move somewhere along the same subway line. First, we did a brief look at places in our area; for less money than we were already paying, we could move to a place that made the mole's hole in Thumbelina look like Trump Palace. In one, I stuck my head out the window and if I strained I could see our current apartment. It made me feel like I would be moving from the manor house to the groundskeeper's cottage.

Since we didn't have the cash to send her to camp, Violet, who was turning six, and I spent the summer looking at apartments in areas along our subway line. I told myself that it was a kind of Real Estate Camp and that if Violet decided to become a broker when she grew up, I would know I'd have myself to thank. On the train, we rehearsed "Always be closing."

We found a bunch of places in the lower part of Washington Heights, but every one of them had something good and something wrong (nice space, view of a wall; great view, not cheap enough for just one bathroom). Paul and I felt determined that if we were going to move from the neighborhood we loved, we'd want to feel like we were getting something better, not just cheaper. More space, two bathrooms, some sort of improvement. And at last we found it. A gigantic apartment about to be gut-renovated, with two bathrooms and giant windows offering full views of the Hudson River and the George Washington Bridge; it was also $1,000 a month cheaper than our current place. As I walked into the apartment and my gaze fell on the windows, I dialed Paul on my cell phone, my hands shaking, to say I'd found it. We were shown the apartment by the super, a lovely Ecuadorian man who, I soon learned, kept an enormous floor-to-ceiling birdcage in the basement and anywhere from five to seven stray cats—this was a pet-friendly building! We were really excited as the time to move got closer. The only question, and one we kind of ignored, was what the neighborhood was like. Twenty blocks up was Washington Heights proper, which was very nice and home to lots of friends. But what was this? Five years back we had seen a listing for the neighborhood, and when I told a friend, a Manhattan assistant DA in narcotics, she said she'd prosecuted a case involving every street in the area. Things had gotten better, though, because the economy had gotten so much worse, and other Upper West Siders had been forced to move there. Another friend had moved up east of there and was quite happy, and we'd heard west was better. We'd be fine. We signed the lease, bought the paints, and waited for our move-in date. On one afternoon when we went up to see how things were going, we walked out of the building to a young thug screaming into his cell phone, "I'm the one out here with the dope *in my hands* and you wanna give me sixty/forty?" (though he said it much more colorfully). We had already committed, and I decided to just block it out. It bothered Paul much more. But we were both a little nervous.

When we moved in, I went to work looking for things to make me feel better about the place (like buildings that didn't have the gang sign for Broadway Locos spray-painted on them). During our first week there, Paul had to go to Los Angeles and I was home alone with Violet and the dogs. It was early evening and there was a huge commotion in front of the building. I could see a crowd of people if I craned my neck out the window, with a lot of shouting, gunshots, and then sirens. I was panicking and shaking and at the same time assuring Violet that everything was fine. I was about to take the dogs out but decided it would be safer to have them crap on the floor.

The next morning I saw one of the guys who worked in the building. "What was that last night?" I asked.

"When?" he said.

"Around six o'clock? There was a lot of shouting and commotion?"

"Oh yeah, that was nothing." He waved it away.

"Some gang retaliation thing, nothing for you to worry about."

My head started calculating the moving costs. I wondered what I could sell to get us out of there: my engagement ring, antique dresser, myself? What do prostitutes make nowadays? Could I just do it with Robert Redford for a million dollars?

In the meantime, I scouted nearby Audubon Terrace—a cul-de-sac of elegant, prewar doorman buildings a few blocks west where the apartments had security. One and a half blocks to my west was the Morris-Jumel Mansion, Manhattan's oldest house, which had once been George Washington's headquarters. It was a bucolic oasis in the midst of a lot of yuck, and we found ourselves spending a lot of time there in workshops. We made weathervanes and mob caps, enjoyed Victorian tea, and in the summer of 2010, Violet upgraded from being a junior realtor and went to a Colonial camp there. On a sweltering Saturday at the end of June when my mom was visiting, we decided to go to Family Day. It was an afternoon of Colonial games, crafts, and an interactive workshop titled "Harriet Tubman, the Underground Railroad, the Cause of Slavery—& Us!"

I thought it would be Violet, my mother, and me, but at the last minute Paul decided to come, too.

For the eleven years Paul and I had been together, we had always been best friends. It was the kind of relationship people remarked upon. But our life together had been hard; it seemed like it went from hard to harder to excruciating and then there would be a small reprieve when we'd catch our breath or get a whiff of hope. There were health issues, deaths, but the most relentless pounding came from our cruddy finances. No matter what we did or how much we cut, we just couldn't break free from the red. And over time, that takes its toll on a relationship. We simply couldn't afford fun. If I got an invitation to a work-related party and felt I needed to go, Paul would stay home with Violet. If Paul had an event, I'd stay home. We rarely used babysitters and since we'd moved up to the hinterlands we didn't have a dog walker anymore, and because someone kept stealing it, we no longer got *The New York Times* delivered. There weren't the kind of cheap but good restaurants we could easily order in from like we did in our old neighborhood (the first time we ordered from the diner around the corner that I thought would be "our place," there was a big hair in my soup). We were now a good half-hour from Violet's school, too far to decide to forgo the subway and hop in a cab if we were running late. I no longer had a washer and dryer in my apartment, so instead of doing the laundry while I did everything else, I now spent a chunk of hours two days a week fighting for a dryer and enduring the other indignities of a shared laundry room. It became something else that I had to work into my already tight schedule. I know this all sounds like middle-class whining, and I really wouldn't have minded any of it, but on top of the new inconveniences was the harshest blow of all. Everything was harder, we had given up so much, and we were still very broke. Nothing had gotten better. And Paul and I were both very angry. And somehow it had turned us against each other.

So when my mother and Violet and I were heading to the Harriet Tubman show, I assumed Paul would skip it. It wasn't something I was looking forward to, the mansion was not air-conditioned, but Violet was a Colonial nut thanks to her American Girl Felicity doll. Paul had been working on a spreadsheet trying to figure out why we didn't have any money. I hated the spreadsheet. Every time he showed it to me I wanted to graffiti a big Anarchy A in a circle on top of it. Our budget wasn't working because we didn't have enough money. I was writing a book, slowly, and magazine articles that often paid three months after the invoices went out. His job paid a decent salary but not enough to cover all of us. That was my answer to everything: We cannot cut one more thing! We cannot live in a cheaper rental, we don't eat out, we don't go to movies, we don't take vacations, the only thing we had that cost money was our choking-the-life-out-of-us debt, and we were stuck with that.

When we started to leave and Paul said he was coming with us, I was a bit shocked, but Violet was thrilled, so off we went.

We walked the two blocks east toward the mansion the way we often do, staggered. Usually I'm ahead of everyone else; Paul and Violet are kind of pokey walkers, while I tend to race. My mother was somewhere in the middle. I was watching the time, because God forbid we would be late for the interactive Harriet Tubman play. Maybe all the good roles would be taken! I walked into the mansion first and registered us all. There were non-Colonial bridge chairs in the parlor, and there was a presentation set up with pictures and charts about the Underground Railroad. We all got seated and a woman talked to us about the story before giving us our parts in the play. They had cards with the character names written on them fastened to strings that we'd wear around our necks. The scene was Harriet putting slaves in a wagon under some goods that needed to cross a bridge. At the other side the slaves could get out and be free. There were guards and helpers in addition to the big-name lead parts. Paul was a guard, my mom and Violet were slaves, and I was a helper—my job was to sing to distract Paul from looking into the wagon and finding the slaves. It all went off without a hitch; my awful singing saved countless lives and after a few more activities we were free to leave. Our plan was to separate; Violet, my mom, and I were going to my aunt Mattie's, where my brother and nieces were about to arrive, and Paul would go home, presumably to work on his spreadsheet, and then come have dinner with us later. We walked out the gate and down toward the street.

"Okay," I said, "I guess we'll go, then." Paul was staring past me. He mumbled something.

"What?" I said.

"That dog is still there." (Cue the bionic sound from *The Six Million Dollar Man* as I move my head around in slow motion to see The Dog.)

Tied to a street sign was a chestnut-colored pit bull. Or, really, a pit bull mix. For a dog in our neighborhood, which was full of tough pooches, he didn't look that pitty or bully at all to me.

"What do you mean, 'still there'?" I asked, walking slowly toward the dog.

Paul made a strange guttural sound. He later said that at the moment he pictured himself like Mel Brooks spinning down the spiral hurricane in *High Anxiety*.

"What?" I said. I hadn't seen the dog when we'd gone in over an hour before. I had been practically sprinting to the door of the mansion and I wasn't looking. Meanwhile, Paul had been taking his time.

There was a mixing bowl near the dog containing a few drops of water. The dog was very excited when I started walking toward him, leaping and trying to bark, but unable to—his throat was so dry only a whisper would come out.

"I'm getting him more water." I picked up the bowl and walked back to the mansion to get some. I approached the Colonial Day delegates.

"There's a pit bull tied up out front—do you know anything about him?" I asked them.

"Oh, no," said a diminutive scullery maid, "I'm afraid of dogs."

"Well, he's tied up, so I just want to see if he belongs to someone in here," I said, filling the bowl with water as cold as I could get.

They all regarded me as Colonial-era people would a curious interloper from the twenty-first century.

I came back out and the dog lapped up every drop of the water, almost gasping with relief like the Tin Man when he gets his oil. He then took a giant pee.

A woman came out of an apartment building. "Is he yours?" she asked.

"No, we just saw him here," I said. "We were in the mansion."

"He's been out here since about six o'clock this morning, maybe before that." It was one-thirty.

"I brought him the water," she said, "and I called the city, but no one's come."

At this point he was sitting nicely and I was standing by him. The sun was hot.

"I'm going to move him into the shade," I said. Paul and my mother both looked at me skeptically.

I undid the leash that was knotted around the sign. It was thick with a very heavy hook that went to his enormous collar. I took him down the street into the shade and when I tried to tie him again he whimpered and jumped up on me, licking my face.

"I'm not leaving you here, I promise," I assured him.

"Oh, great," Paul muttered.

"You were the one who pointed him out," I said.

"I know," Paul said, "and if I could take it back . . ."

I glared at him. "Go home. I'll figure this out on my own."

"I'm not leaving . . . I'm not going. I'll stay," he said.

"Well, *we're* not waiting here," my mother said. I told her to take Violet to Mattie's and I'd call her when . . . when . . . what? I had no idea what I was doing.

The woman who'd brought out the water bowl had just started complaining about the city's lack of response to her call when a police car on patrol rolled by. She started waving frantically at it and it slowed down and reversed.

"Are you looking for us?" she asked the policeman, smiling and straightening out her shirt.

"Nooooo," the cop in the driver's seat said slowly.

"Oh," she said, disappointment lacing her words, "because I called 311 about this dog being left here."

"Um, we're not animal control," the police officer said, a little sarcastically. He looked like Louis Gossett, Jr., and I was waiting for him to tell me not to eyeball him.

The woman turned away from him, and her face erupted in rage. She shouted a blue streak. "What are you cops good for?" she demanded, heavy on the colorful language so that everyone would know how angry she was. She looked to me for agreement.

I quickly glanced away from her and sidestepped a few feet over. Big coward that I am, I was not about to receive her comment. I did not want to be associated with this instigator. I loved cops, especially in this neighborhood, and I didn't want to piss them off.

I started petting the dog.

The cop got out of the car. His name tag said "Lorenz." *Here we go,* I thought, *he's going to arrest her for disturbing the peace.*

"I could take the dog," he said to me, "but if I bring him to animal control, they're going to kill him, you understand?"

"Oh yeah, no, I agree," I said. "I do dog rescue, so I'm going to try and figure something out."

"You see," he enunciated to Paul, "you don't want me taking the dog, right? Because he's not going to live."

"That's fine," Paul said, nodding. He and I were both law-abiders. Miss Foul-Mouth was on her own.

She walked over to where I was petting the dog, looking more visibly upset. "I can't believe this—I had a drink with that cop and he's acting like he's never seen me before."

Ah, okay, so this was not about the dog. Her "boy-friend" was dissing her. I took a look at her. She was fairly nondescript with salt-and-pepper not-quite-shoulder-length hair and a shapeless body. At this moment she was wearing a stained T-shirt and rumpled, baggy Bermuda shorts. I wasn't quite sure why she'd want the cop to re-member her.

She was shaking her head in disbelief and began stringing together expletives the likes of which I hadn't heard since my father came upon our broken boiler in the winter of 1976. Not getting any response from me, she picked up the bowl and turned to go home.

"Maybe you could leave the water bowl for now?" I said. "I'll bring it to you later."

She put it back down. "Forget it, just throw it out when you're done." She spat.

For the third or maybe fourth time the cop explained to us why he wouldn't be taking this dog and why we shouldn't even have called the city, and I quietly responded that *we* hadn't done anything. His partner, a younger woman, got out of the car and came over.

"Seems like a real nice dog," she said, contemplatively. "My kids want a dog, but I'm not home during the day."

"Are you a nice dog?" Lorenz asked the dog. "Huh?"

I wanted to tell the dog not to answer without the presence of an attorney, but he was already crying at the cop to be petted.

"He's a nice dog," Lorenz said, finally smiling, revealing gold-rimmed front teeth. He seemed to be considering taking him, too. I wondered what it was about this dog that made everyone who met him feel responsible for him or at least bound to come up with a reason why they couldn't be responsible for him.

I took the opportunity to snap his photo on my BlackBerry and post it on Facebook and Twitter with a message: *Help me find a home for this sweet abandoned pit bull!* Then I e-mailed it to all of my rescue and dog friends, including Ken, a writer who worked with pit bull rescue in New Orleans. He was originally from New York, and he remained connected in the world of dog owners here.

The cops stayed for a while. I think they wanted to find out what would happen to the dog, plus it was such a hot, slow Saturday and we were in the shadow of these ancient trees that George Washington could have taken shade under.

I started getting responses from people on Twitter, which was like a high-tech twilight bark from *101*

Dalmatians. The cops got back in their car, wished us luck, and slowly drove off.

And now we were alone.

"What should we name him?" I mused.

Paul did the thing where his neck dissolves and his head tips over.

"You know we can't bring that dog home," he said.

"I know!" I said. It wasn't just that we already had three dogs, we had three poorly behaved dogs. They were aggressive toward outsiders and would surely get themselves eaten by this sweet fellow.

Paul softened. "We could call him . . ." He started looking around.

I looked at the signs directing visitors to the mansion. "Stephen or Jumel or Roger—"

"Not Roger," Paul responded. Roger was Paul's father's name and the name he had wanted for our baby if it was a boy.

"How about Morris?" I asked.

"Good."

"Hello, Mr. Morris!" I said in my high-pitched dog voice. He leaped and wailed; we'd chosen correctly.

"He's a great dog. Maybe we could trade him for our three," Paul said.

"Trade with who? The street sign?"

"We need to get him more water."

"And we should get him some food," I added. "I'll go."

"No. I'll go, I want to get something to eat, too," he said. "And Morris is your dog."

"Fine," I agreed.

"Do you want something to eat?"

"No, just water."

He walked toward St. Nicholas Avenue and turned right. I sat down next to Morris and he started pawing at me. I thought maybe I would walk him. I undid his leash and took him down the hill to the grass, where he peed for a very long time, and then walked him a bit farther, to where he pooped. He must not have wanted to go where we were sitting; he was what my dad would call "a clean dog." Why would someone give up a fellow like this? I must ask this question a thousand times a year. I knew a woman who rescued pit bulls and she told me that often if an owner got the dog to fight and the dog wasn't aggressive enough, they'd get rid of it. As far as I could see, this guy was as sweet as could be. I sat down with him and we began to talk.

"You from around here?" He started licking me. "Mmm, salty!" He licked my face and my eye. "Morris! I've got mascara on, that's not going to taste good." He tipped his head. He had such a funny big skull and an old-timey face. I started to sing "Ol' Man River" in my deepest voice. And Morris sang along. More like howled, but still. I stopped singing and he stopped howling. I started singing "Happy Together" by the Turtles, and he crooned again. I broke into a medley of the worst songs of the '60s, '70s, and '80s, also known as my gym play-list. He sang when I sang, and stopped when I stopped.

"You are a trick dog!" I said. He gave me several kisses and put his paws on my bare thighs.

"Ow!" I said. "Watch the nails!" I picked up his paws to get them off me and then I saw them. There were cigarette burn marks on the top of one paw, and when I looked at the others, I noticed identical marks.

"Oh, no, no, no," I murmured to myself, and pulled him onto my lap and hugged and held him. He let me, too, and every so often he'd turn around and slurp my face and then let me go back to scratching behind his ears and kissing the top of his head.

I suddenly wondered if the person who had tied him up out here was getting him away from whoever was abusing him. I would never know.

My BlackBerry chimed and it was an e-mail back from Ken. He had forwarded my plea to some people here in New York, including a very famous novelist who rescued dogs, and told me he'd call me if anyone came through. He also said that under no circumstances should I bring the dog to the Center for Animal Care and Control (CACC)—the city shelter. They would definitely put him down.

I checked Twitter, and several people had recommended possible shelters and rescue groups. Being a part of a rescue group, I knew those things were not immediate. You contacted someone over e-mail and then waited for the person to get back to you and so on. It was a good long-term plan, but I didn't have long-term. I Googled the shelters and called each one. Mostly I got voicemail, and before I could even leave a message I'd hear, "We do not take pit bulls." The one or two that did take pits were filled to capacity. This was a new dog problem, one I hadn't encountered before personally.

Paul came walking up the street with grocery bags and jugs of water. He poured the water into the now empty bowl and Morris lapped it up, and Paul filled it again and Morris drank it again.

I looked in the bag. There were three giant cans of Alpo, which I thought of as the McDonald's of dog food (they love it, but it's bad for them).

"It was the only food with a pull top," Paul explained. "We don't have a can opener out here."

"It's fine," I said, "especially if it's his last meal."

I opened one can and piled it onto the plastic grocery bag; Morris inhaled it.

"Should we give him another one?" I asked. It reminded me of when Violet was a newborn, and I'd call Paul at work and ask him if I should feed her again. Neither one of us knew anything, but it seemed like if we put our heads together we would have the best shot at not killing her.

"I guess so."

I poured another can down and he ate it with the same vigor.

"Okay, take a rest, Morris," I said, petting him, and then told Paul that I was going to call Ann.

Ann is a good friend of mine who lives in Connecticut. She and I had bonded over being dog crazies (we both had three), and we'd recently talked over lunch about a woman she knew who bordered on animal hoarder—she literally took in every dog that crossed her path and was vehemently against euthanizing. Ann and I had a long discussion about whether or not it was actually kinder to re-home an old or very nutty dog or put it to sleep. It was a big debate in the dog rescue community. We always try to do what's best for the dog, but sometimes you just don't really know what that is. So I called Ann and told her the story of Morris and asked if she thought the hoarder might take him. She said she might, but at the very least Ann could probably take the dog overnight if we couldn't find anyplace else. The problem was she was going to a fund-raiser and would be out until about eight, so she couldn't pick him up. Paul and I actually had my mother's car, but I really didn't want to saddle Ann with this dog . . . yet.

People walked by, averting their eyes. A man from one of the beautiful brownstones across the street came out of his apartment and walked over. He'd seen the dog early in the morning, too.

"Wow, she's a beauty!" he remarked, getting a closer look.

"He," I said.

"Oh," he laughed, "sorry! I mean, uh, no offense!"

Paul talked to him while I called more shelters. The guy kept complimenting Morris, and I saw the same inner dialogue as with everyone else: *Could I take this dog?*

He said he had a brother in Pennsylvania with a lot of land whose dog had recently passed away. He went inside to call him and see if maybe he'd want Morris.

It's a funny thing I'd noticed while living in New York City for twenty-five years. When something happened in public, a person falling or a bicycle rider being hit by a car or an animal tied up outside of someplace for what seemed like too long, a cloud of people would gather and sort of wait for a custodian of the situation to present himself. Sometimes it was the first person on the scene or someone who was more "take charge" than others or one who just wasn't racing to get to work. And then the cloud would evaporate. Sort of like, "Okay, you got this? Then I'm going to return to my day." I'd been on both sides. I'd been walking one day when a large woman slipped on the ice, and two men and I rushed over to her. They helped her up, but she felt more comfortable with me walking her. I'd also rushed into scenes where there was someone on a cell phone calling for help and someone sitting with the person who had passed out or gotten hit and there was no need for me. More often than not, if there was an animal, I became the pack leader.

The previous winter, Paul and I had been walking on Broadway and noticed that a swarm of people were congregating around two dogs tied up in front of a grocery store. A woman came out of the store with food for them; she said that they'd been out there for *several hours*! The other people were discussing whether or not they'd been abandoned. I didn't think they were. They had no identification tags, but they had rabies chips and they were wearing fancy coats. Maybe, someone conjectured, the person who tied them up went shopping and died. Or, someone else thought, fainted. Or maybe they'd been abducted by aliens. The woman who brought out the food was now wondering which one of us would take them; she couldn't because she had nine cats. This was not a surprising detail to me.

"I might . . ." I said tentatively, and looked up to Paul, who was outside the circle of people, shaking his head no very hard, mouthing, "We have four dogs," and holding up four fingers. (It was true, we did have a foster at the time.) I nodded back to him. "Right!" I mouthed. "I know." He nodded again at me with a faint smile, then mimed, "If you take them . . ." and pointed at himself and finger-shot himself in the head.

Such a kidder!

There are people who begrudgingly rescue animals and there are people who take animals and try to force them into being rescued, even if they aren't lost. I called the phone number of the vet on the rabies tags; it was Saturday, though, and there was no live person. A couple of police officers walked up and said they could take the dogs and then they said they couldn't take the dogs and then some guy walking by said to them, "Why don't you fight some real crime!" (There is always one loudmouth who announces this to cops in New York City.) And in the midst of all of this, a man came out of a bank.

"What's going on?" he asked, untying their leashes from the pole.

"These dogs have been left here for hours!" yelled a woman who'd arrived about thirty seconds before.

"They're my dogs! It hasn't been hours," he said, not as defensively as I would have.

The cops gave him a stern talking-to and we left.

Sadly, no one would be coming out of the bank for Morris, so I was his keeper and, begrudgingly, so was Paul.

Paul pulled a box of Kashi snack bars out of the grocery bag.

"I got these for you."

"Oh, thanks." I took the box and studied them. "Mmm, chocolate almond."

"It was either those or a Cuban sandwich."

I smiled. One good thing about being with someone for a long time is that he knows what to get you in a weird supermarket. I was a "bar" eater. I was murderously hard on myself workout- and diet-wise, and my husband knew this. He was very much the opposite of me in this way, and though early in our relationship he once tried to force-feed me a Godiva pumpkin truffle because I refused to try it, he's always been pretty understanding of my neuroses (well, this one, anyway). He also knew I was afraid to eat in restaurants that looked even the slightest bit dirty. Or stay over at people's houses. And despite the fact that he liked staying at strange people's weird, smelly homes and eating in funky bug-riddled cafés, we didn't do it. Because he valued my comfort almost as much as I did. That was not something small to me.

"I never saw these before," I said, reading the box of bars and biting into one. "Oh, they're good. Excellent find, honey, thank you."

"Of course."

It was a very small moment of exchanged kindness. But for the first time in a long time, I felt like my hackles were down.

Paul sat on the ground next to me. Morris put his paws on his shoulder. He gently corrected him: "Now,

Morris, you must put your best feet forward, but not on people's heads."

"I think he's showing you his paws," I said.

Paul looked at them and shook his head in sadness and disgust. "Poor Morris."

I kept checking my BlackBerry and looking at the responses; so many people were trying to help. The problem was we needed something immediately. We needed to get him housed before nightfall or we were looking at the city shelter. I couldn't bear to think of that possibility, but I had to be pragmatic. Deep down I knew there was no way I was going to be putting him in that shelter, but somehow I had to project that I was entertaining that possibility or *some* people would not be so helpful.

"You know you can leave," I said to Paul again.

"I'm not leaving," he said.

It was about three p.m., and we'd been here with Morris for a couple of hours. I realized my own dogs were home alone . . . Home alone with air-conditioning on, plenty of food and water in their bowls . . . lucky dogs.

. . .

A woman I didn't know who had heard about Morris through Twitter called me. She was a "friend to dogs" in New Jersey and knew about a place in SoHo that took pit bulls. She offered to call on my behalf. Since my BlackBerry battery was dwindling, I said yes, please.

Paul was really liking Morris. The dog avocation was wholly mine, and Paul was just an innocent, but mostly amenable, passive bystander. I walked and fed and vetted our dogs, and when a needy one popped up, it was in my inbox. Paul did really want a big dog, though. Spinone Italiano was his breed of choice, and though it sounded like a Venetian confection, it was actually a sort of wolfhoundish-looking dog, somewhat on the rare side and not really a breed requiring rescue. I knew he would have wanted us to take Morris if our home wasn't already so overrun with dogs (which was my fault). We had our original Boston terrier, Beatrice, a pretty well-trained, if slightly indifferent, housebroken female, and Wisteria and Fiorello, the puppies of a foster-gone-wrong. Dahlia, their late mother, was supposed to be a sickly, spayed senior, instead she was an unspayed pregnant senior.

Wisteria and Fiorello, for lack of a better term, were feral. Okay, they were not that bad. They were very sweet at home—affectionate, cuddly—and they both had really good breath. Unfortunately, they seemed to be born with the gene resistant to housebreaking, though I hadn't been perfect about training them. In my defense, it is hard to housebreak a dog (let alone two at one time) in a New York City apartment. When you're housebreaking a dog, the key is to get them out in a timely manner. If you live in an apartment on the sixteenth floor, that's about as easy as it sounds. I would sense that they needed to go out, and by the time I got their collars and leashes on and pressed the elevator button and waited for it and took it down to the lobby, it was no longer timely. More like it was timely to get a roll of paper towels and some Fantastik.

Somehow I housebroke Beatrice with no problem in a very short period of time right before I went on bed rest for my pregnancy. It's like I told her, "You go to the bathroom outside, not inside." And she anwered, "Got it." Whereas Wisteria and Fiorello were told, shown, taken outside with paper towels with their pee on them to show them where it went. I did a puppet show and a Power-Point demonstration and they still didn't get it. They'd go out for long, long walks and come back inside and pee on the rug. Wisteria would look at me like, *"Well, I don't understand what you want from me! This thick woolen rug is just the same as the stuff outside, only it's inside and I can get the opportunity to keep smelling it for weeks."* And Fiorello, the little gangsta, will pee while you're watching him and then deny it. He has an expression of shock on his face all the time, like he's constantly being framed for something. He growled at my niece one summer (I thought she was looking particularly menacing in her pink flowered bathing suit) and we put him behind a gate. The whole time he stared at me and I could hear his Jimmy Cagney voice saying, *"You gotta get me outta here! I'm dyin' in this place."* So, yeah, in addition to the not being housebroken, they walked on leashes like a gang of elephants if elephants yanked at your arm and barked at and tried to attack every other elephant they passed.

That is why we couldn't take this sweet pit bull into our house. It would've been the tipping point . . . for our sanity.

The Friend to Dogs called me back and said she'd spoken to this place, Animal Farm or whatever it was called, and if we could get there by five o'clock, they would do a personality assessment, and if he was okay, they would take him. The test was to make sure he was not aggressive, and I knew he'd do well with that. Morris was a little pushy and licky, but he'd been very easygoing for the couple hours that we'd been with him.

"Oh my God, okay! Can you please tell them we'll be there?" She agreed and we hung up. Then I realized that although we had my mother's car, she had the keys, on the Upper East Side. It was three-fifteen; it would take a half-hour for her to get to us and an hour to get downtown. In other words, we'd just about make it.

I called my mother and said I'd come get the keys, and the routine began. I realized it would take too long and asked her to bring the keys to me, and then my mother said, "Oh, okay, but we aren't ready to come back there, Violet's still playing with her cousins, so maybe I'll leave her here and just bring you the keys." Then my aunt Mattie said, "I'll drive you over, cab fare is twenty-five dollars." An argument ensued: "You don't have to drive me." "I'm driving you, so hang up so I can call the garage."

"Okay, Mattie is driving her here with the keys," I told Paul, who'd heard the whole thing.

We waited for my mother.

"Maybe you should tutor him for his test," I suggested to Paul.

"Sit, sit, sit, sit," he commanded, and Morris didn't move. "Write that down: 'Doesn't sit.'"

"But wait," I said, and started singing "Do You Know the Way to San Jose." And right on cue Morris "whoa whoa whoa'd" along.

Paul laughed.

"He sings!" I said.

"Perfect," Paul responded, and to Morris he said in a *Broadway Danny Rose* voice, "You're hired!"

I'd written and spoken about fostering dogs, and something I always said was that a stray/shelter/surrendered dog's personality takes time to discover, a couple of weeks maybe. In the case of Morris, here is what we knew: He was a pit bull mix, not a very big dog at all, and on the thin side. He was outfitted in a collar that was four inches wide and fastened too tightly, and tethered to a hook that was about the size we had used on our horse leads to keep them from running off while the horses were grazing. He had been tied to a NO PARKING sign by someone between Friday night and Saturday morning. As the spot he was in slowly went from early-morning summer shade to blazing-hot sun, he'd been dehydrated and hungry. He wasn't aggressive toward us; on the contrary, he was gentle and pleading. When Violet was there he was completely sweet to her, and the coming and goings of people didn't spook him. If he was just "acting" like he was a nice dog and was secretly a vicious beast, I was very relieved and hoped he'd keep it up, at least until I could find him a bed for the night. If anyone asked, he was the sweetest dog I'd ever met.

I kept calling my mother for status updates on her location. I was getting really anxious, because it was Saturday and the traffic getting downtown was a big unknown. We really didn't have time to spare, and it was taking her longer than a half-hour to get to us. I went to where her car was and waited so that the minute she got there she could toss me the keys, I could jump into the car and go pick up Paul and Morris, briefly stopping to switch places because Paul was more of a driver than I was, and then scurry downtown, bring Morris inside; they would test him, love him, take him, we'd go home and I'd make the chicken fajitas I'd begun preparing.

I believe the phrase was "easy peasy."

Except it was getting later and there was still no Mom and Mattie.

At four-twenty they came ambling up. Mattie was not a speed demon in her best driving days, and now she's the butt of my jokes. "If you hit that pedestrian, all you'd do is shove him a bit." We'd recently gone to Costco in New Jersey and she'd refused to go down a steep hill because she thought her car would flip over (though the cars ahead of us seemed to be managing just fine). We had to keep driving until we found a flat street.

I grabbed the keys from my mother and zipped over to Paul, trying to make up some lost time. He and Morris were waiting.

We scooted around until Paul was in the driver's seat. Morris got in the back and we were off.

Since we'd moved farther uptown, we'd been trying to master the art of getting places without taking the endless avenues. We could go down the West Side Highway very well, but getting places on the East Side was more complicated. There was the Harlem River Drive, which seemed to work well, but in my mind it was like Platform 9¾, where Harry Potter and his friends gather to take the Hogwarts Express. I could never manage to find it except by accident, and sometimes I'd be on it when I thought I was on the FDR Drive, the East Side version of the West Side Highway. We were at this strange place by the mansion, this Edgecomb Avenue thing that exists only uptown, and for some reason you can see Yankee Stadium in the Bronx from there. It's all very difficult for me to understand, and apparently for Paul also, because we were driving for fifteen minutes and still hadn't gotten anywhere. The clock was ticking. We did our husband-and-wife bickering about directions, which was rare since we didn't have a car, but we had been married, so we had the tools for the argument. I just kept thinking that we were not going to get there in time and we'd be ending up with Morris and then Paul would be enraged at me and I'd have to take Morris to the Center for Animal Care and Control and then I'd be furious with Paul.

It had been a long day and it still wasn't over. Both of us had adrenaline pumping; contrary to popular opinion, this doesn't make your car move faster through bumper-to-bumper traffic, which is what we ended up in when we finally got onto the FDR Drive.

Somehow—*somehow*—we got downtown, but not before five. In fact, we were sitting in traffic for several minutes just a few blocks away from the place, so I told Paul I'd take Morris over and at whatever month he managed to get out of the traffic, he could meet me out front.

It was a strange thing to be walking this dog who wasn't mine through SoHo. For a little while I got to try on the persona of being a pit bull owner. The responses were very different from the ones I got for walking a pod of snapping terriers. A Keanu Reeves doppelgänger commented, "Hey, beautiful dog." I thought a pit bull owner who looked like me would seem like a rescuer, since I certainly wasn't using him for dogfighting, what with my little cotton sundress and hair in a high ponytail. And being a big-dog owner seemed to have a cachet that being a small-dog owner didn't. Like driving a city bus instead of a Prius. But maybe that big-dog-owner credibility just came from having to pick up bigger dumps.

A rush of relief swept over me when I got inside the place and found it was open and pretty and air-conditioned and they were expecting me. They had no idea what I was talking about with the five-o'clock deadline. I was just too grateful to be annoyed about the seconds I lost off my life worrying about making it here in time.

A woman came down some spiral stairs and greeted Morris. I told her his whole sad story, and he was his usual (well, what was usual for the last several hours) sweet self. She took him away, and I waited and looked around. A couple had come in to adopt a dog they must have met earlier in the day and went off to think over. I felt their excitement and nervousness and listened as they asked questions about feeding and walking and crating. They bought a ton of stuff and were walking out when the woman saw a stuffed purple dinosaur dog toy. "Do you think he might like something like this?" she asked the shelter worker.

"Um, yeah, why not?" she said.

It was very funny to me, like when I had a five-year-old kid and would hear someone with a newborn asking questions that I had once asked that really couldn't possibly make a difference but made me feel better for having asked.

"Will buying this stuffed purple dinosaur make this dog leaving the shelter feel happy and well loved?"

"Should I swaddle my newborn baby in her blanket and then put the little hat on her head, or put the little hat on her head first and then swaddle her?"

Paul came in, triumphant from finding a space on the street right out front. I told him Morris was being assessed and the time was fine, and he rolled his eyes because we needn't have rushed.

We were both feeling a little giddy at having made this happen. I assumed we'd offer a donation and then be done. The woman came back downstairs with Morris.

"He did really well!" she said, petting him. "We would definitely take him."

"Great! Hooray!" I said, and began to gather my things. "You can keep the leash and collar."

"Oh," she said, her face falling, "we can't take him *now*."

Both Paul and I looked puzzled.

"No, we're totally filled to capacity," she said, a bit irritated by the nerve of us to think he was staying. "He will go on our waiting list and when a space opens up, we'll let you know."

"But . . . we need a place for him now," I insisted.

She shrugged. Paul was getting angry with her. "We were told you could take him if we got him here and he was assessed."

"Well," she said, "you were told wrong."

"He's not our dog. We found him abandoned. Tied up on the street," he said.

We might as well have been telling her that we were out of seven-grain bread and her sandwich would have to go on whole wheat.

"Forget it," I said to Paul.

"You can take him to the Center for Animal Care and Control," she offered. "It's on the Upper East Side. You want me to give you the address?"

"No, thanks," I mumbled.

I took Morris's leash back from her and we went outside. As predicted, Paul was raging.

"What the hell was that? What did we rush down here for?"

"I don't know any more than you," I said defensively.

"I'm not angry with you!" he yelled.

We both stood on the sidewalk in silence for what seemed like a very long time. Morris began to pant.

"All right," I said quietly. "Let's just take him to the CACC."

He took a deep breath. "You're not responsible for every dog in the whole world, Julie."

"I know," I said, and I did know . . . sort of.

"I feel like I'm going to pass out," he said. "I need to get something to eat."

"Okay."

"La Esquina is right around the corner. And there's Homoos, that Middle Eastern place."

La Esquina was a Mexican restaurant close to Paul's office, which we were near right then. When Obama was running for president they had the most amazing T-shirts. They were plain on the front and said OBAMA over 08 on the back, like a team shirt, with a little LA ESQUINA on the sleeve. Paul had gotten me one and I loved it, so he went back and got me all the other colors.

"Either one is fine with me," I said.

We got back in the car and my phone battery was very low but I didn't have a car charger. "Can I use your phone? I want to try Ann again."

I took his phone and got her voicemail.

"Hi, it's me calling again. I'm on Paul's cell because mine is dead. The place we thought would take Morris isn't taking him because of some baloney, though he did really well on his assessment test. Anyway, I don't know if you have any ideas, but we're in my mom's car in SoHo if you get this and can call me back." I gave her the number as Paul pulled the car into a space. He went for food while I sat in the car with Morris with the air-conditioning running. I felt numb and empty. I petted Morris without looking at his eyes.

I noticed my mother's charger was in the car—it fit Paul's phone, so I was able to connect his now dwindling phone to it and started checking my Twitter and Facebook to see if anyone had responded to my posts. It rang, and it was Ann.

"Hi," I said.

"What's going on?" she asked. She was calling me from the fund-raiser. I updated her about Morris in as much of a nutshell as I could, and without a thought she said, "I will take him."

"Oh, Ann!" I said, trying not to cry.

"I'm done here at seven-thirty. I probably can't drive all the way into the city but I could meet you halfway."

"You don't have to! We'll drive him to you."

She was taking Morris off our hands and also trying to save us from having to drive him all the way to Connecticut. What an amazing friend. I told her we'd be thrilled to take him to her door; it was about six forty-five now, and we'd get him to her by eight-thirty or nine. I was so happy I wanted to jump through the phone and kiss her. The whole day had been one disappointing blow after another. No good deed had gone unpunished, until now.

Paul got back in the car with the most sizzlingly delectable-smelling Mexican food, and to judge from the size of the bag, lots of it. I suddenly realized I was light-headed from hunger, something I wouldn't have allowed myself to address if we were taking Morris to the shelter. Not like it was a conscious protest or anything, I just can't eat when I'm scared.

"Guess what?" I said to Paul as I took the bag from him. "Ann's going to take Morris!"

"Really? Oh, that's great!" he said, buoyant.

"I'll drop you off at home and drive him up there," I offered.

"No, I don't mind going up there . . . now that I've got some food." He opened his burrito and squirted on hot sauce. "Is she going to keep him?"

"Maybe. Probably not. She has some ideas of some places he can go, though . . . up near her."

"Wow, that is awesome."

We both focused on eating, and Morris was quite interested. I took a bit of chicken and rinsed it off with water and gave it to him.

"That's all you're getting, buddy," I told him. "You're going to my good friend's house tonight and I don't want you to be all gassy."

"God, I'm so relieved," Paul said, looking out the window.

"So. Am. I."

"The idea," he said, "of having gone through all of that just to bring him to the shelter he would've gone to if we'd never found him . . ."

"I know," I said, though what I was thinking was that we never would have done it. There's a children's book that Violet loved when she was little called *McDuff Moves In*. It's about a stray dog that ends up with a couple named Fred and Lucy, and they're going to take him to the city shelter. They're in their car driving him around, but they're not getting any closer. Fred is going around in circles, because, well, he doesn't want to take this dog to the shelter and, guess what, neither does Lucy. So they drive back home and keep him (after feeding him sausages and vanilla pudding and giving him a coconut bath). Anyway, that's what I kept thinking about. Paul and I would just keep stalling until we found a solution.

Paul opened the windows and the moon roof and turned off the air-conditioning.

As the late-day sky was turning the mango, raspberry, and lemon tones of a swirly summer Popsicle, a large billboard in lilac neon lit up above us. Some of the heat that had made the day feel like an angry overblown balloon was taking leave and a breeze passed through the car. We sat for a minute and just watched the city go by, momentarily not feeling like a victim of it.

"This is the first dinner out alone we've had in months," he said, chomping on some quesadilla. He tore off a piece and passed it to me and I ate it out of his fingers.

"And we're alone," I said, "sort of." I looked back at Morris.

"At least he isn't interrupting our conversation."

"No, he just is our conversation."

"Should we go?" I asked.

"Yeah," Paul said. He looked at me. "Thank you for having dinner with me."

I smiled at him.

I programmed Ann's address into the GPS, and Paul started the car. We drove and chatted, going through the day over and over, and feeling a bit smug and vindicated that although we'd been turned away by the SoHo place, Morris would be going to one of the loveliest homes in one of the most bucolic parts of Connecticut. Ha, ha, ha. We WON!

We pulled into Ann's driveway at about eight forty-five, and she came out to meet us. We let Morris out of the car and Ann's dogs gave him a few *"Who the heck are you?"* woofs and he responded, *"I'm Morris from Manhattan."* There were some territory issues, but for the most part it was okay. Ann described his arrival later:

> *He began to urinate as soon as he had all four paws on driveway. Julie, Paul, and I discussed his rescue. We discussed the dog's future. We discussed the weather, and the traffic on the drive up. Morris continued to urinate. We discussed astrology and exchanged our childbirth stories and admired photos of each other's children.*

Morris was still weeing, glancing up at us apologetically from time to time. I admired their car. Finally, after approximately ten minutes, Morris decided to change it up. His spine, which had been inverted dramatically during the lengthy urine drainage, was now humped and seizing. He had diarrhea. He began the diarrhea release on the driveway and in a show of startling athleticism, he was able to move, humping and squirting, to the newly planted flower bed twenty feet away. There he decided to turn the fecal output into a fine spray. Several minutes later he finished voiding his bowels and Julie and Paul told me about the three giant cans of Alpo they'd fed him and pretended this wasn't a practical joke.

We sat outside on her patio while the dogs frolicked. One of her dogs, Holly, seemed to really take a shine to Morris, but Daphne seemed to want him gone.

I told Ann about the weird woman who'd gotten so

mad when the cop hadn't recognized her even though they had had a drink together. "Maybe she put out for him," Ann joked. "No one gets that mad over not being recognized from a drink." Paul and I laughed so hard we cried. There was a tremendous amount of relief there, for Morris and for us.

It was getting late and Paul was being eaten alive by mosquitoes, so I squeezed Ann and thanked her again. Morris seemed to want to get back in the car with us, but it was probably because he thought he had died and gone to heaven there.

The trip back was peaceful, and we felt as though we'd done something very good for this dog, and at the same time, for ourselves.

"Do you think Ann will keep him?" Paul wondered again.

"I doubt it," I said. "She was telling me about this amazing shelter up here called the Simon Foundation. They take pit bulls and work with them and train them. I think she may end up bringing him there." I knew if Ann brought him, she'd have to sponsor him, but I also knew that she wouldn't hesitate. Her generous spirit never faltered. She is an endless source of inspiration to me.

"That was kind of fun," I said. "When was the last time we rode alone in a car together?"

"I think when you were pregnant?"

"Too long." I shook my head. It was so easy for us to get wrapped up in the crap of our lives. We seemed to only come together to wring our hands about money woes and overall feelings of failure. Anytime one of us wanted to talk, it was to highlight some impending doom, and then, not surprisingly, we weren't interested in coming together at all. This day with Morris, we came together for someone else. We had a difficult, but not impossible, goal and we achieved it.

"I'm so glad you stayed with me today." I really was.

Paul was looking at the road. "I had a feeling," he said tentatively, "that if I left you, that would've been it."

I knew exactly what he meant. Our lives were filled with moments in which choices presented themselves; I did not think it was an accident that it was Paul who pointed out that the dog was still out there. He knew I wouldn't leave the dog. That was something he always said about me, and maybe that day Morris was our marriage counselor.

It was such a cliché about being married for a long time, with kids and dogs and such a busy life that you needed to make time for the two of you. We always dismissed that as a luxury that we couldn't afford instead of seeing it as something vital, like our food and shelter. Paul and I used to walk along Riverside Drive and pick the buildings we wanted to live in, astonishingly handsome prewar buildings with their carved gargoyles and angels. I always marveled at the ones that had been in direct winds and weather so much that their cornices softened, looking more like snow sculptures than concrete. It is frighteningly easy for a solid relationship to erode under the beatings of everyday struggles.

But if you wanted to, you could restore yourselves. We were both still under there.

We got home and the house was dark, Violet and my mother long sleeping. We ate some of the chocolate chip cookies my mom had brought, and looked out the window at the boats sailing down the Hudson with their night lights on and the George Washington Bridge with its diamond necklaces. It wasn't all bad. Sometimes you just had to stop and look. Maybe you'd find a dog there. Maybe yourself.

2.

My Darling Clementine

Violet's new school commute took about a half hour on a packed subway. Her school was in our old neighborhood on the Upper West Side, near my gym. So after dropping her off, I'd work out and take the subway back home, where I'd walk the dogs and do my work and any housework that needed doing. If it was a wash day, that would take a few hours in a laundry room in the basement, with six washers and dryers (at least one permanently out of order) shared among the roughly eighty apartments. I'd walk the dogs again and head down to pick Violet up from school. The subway rides were one of the major drags of city life; it was just not a nice way for a little kid to start the day. Rushing, pushing, intransigent crowds, frequently no seats, all made that much more difficult when you are six. I felt guilty that because of our finances, we'd moved from a place where we could easily take a bus or a cab and sometimes walk to school, to this. I did everything I could to make it more pleasant—asking people to move a little closer together so Violet could have a seat, playing games (I spy with my little eye someone who is drooling!), reading to her, bringing her fun snacks—but it was never going to be more than a sow's rump.

The subway station where we came out at 3:50 p.m. was a frequent congregation spot for drug dealers and their customers—right on the stairs! They would walk down into the crowd and hand pills to someone and keep going down the stairs or go back up. I was incensed and tried to report it, but it was a little bit of a moving target, and really our only option was to steer clear of the trouble and pray for a windfall that would let us move back to our old neighborhood.

By the time the holidays approached, it was beginning to feel like everything I did was an attempt to make up for the miserable place we were in. I was overjoyed when we were invited to a Christmas Eve party at our friend's stately Chelsea brownstone. I grew up with this friend's family, and they all sang and played piano by the grand Christmas tree at their annual party. It felt like something out of *A Christmas Carol*.

Unfortunately, the morning of the party Violet awoke with a fever, and since there was also a terrible ice storm, we were grounded. During the day I'd gone out looking for some Christmas chocolates, the little foil-wrapped Santas and balls and bells and kisses that to me made Christmas great—or, if Christmas stank, you could at least eat a bunch of chocolate. I took a walk ten blocks up and down and couldn't find them anywhere in the neighborhood. Chicken feet? Yes. Chocolate snowmen? Nope.

I have a tendency to harp on things, kind of like . . . a harpy. I guess Paul was tired of hearing me complain about the lack of Christmas chocolates and felt that he would be able to find them. If you were betting on one of us to be a sweets hunter and gatherer, you'd definitely put your money on my diabetic husband, who over the course of our marriage had quested for a certain Entenmann's Brownie Crumb Ring that, I think through his sheer force of will, had been brought out of retirement.

A grim-mouthed Paul put on his coat and hat and boots and went out into the hall while I mumbled about confectionary injustices. A minute after the door closed I heard a loud not-joking yelling in the hall. I opened the door and the three dogs careened out. Paul was by the elevator and approximately nine cops were dragging a man in his underwear down the stairs. The cops yelled at us to get back inside our apartment, the dogs tried to bite everyone, and I was so scared that I was shaking like a cartoon character. I picked up the dogs in my arms and we went back inside. Paul angrily snapped at me, "Why did you open the door?"

"I thought someone had hurt you," I retorted.

He held me and said it was okay. But it wasn't.

The next day I joked about it: "It's just not Christmas until your upstairs neighbor gets dragged out of his apartment in his underwear by nine cops." And P.S., no chocolates.

I kept saying, "It's going to get better," and "Everything's going to work out." But I didn't really know how it would. I just had belief and a little bit of Scarlett O'Hara determination. (Did I mention that I have a flair for the dramatic?) And lo, about a year after we moved to Villa Complainia and through a lot of hard work, the angel of good luck shone mercifully down upon us and we got a couple of good rains after a long, long, long, long drought. Finally, we were out of debt, in demand, flush, solvent, in the black, Bob was indeed our uncle. And as God was mah witness, I would nevah go hungry agin!

It was a very happy autumn, and we headed into the holidays with a vigor and determination for everything to be SO UNBELIEVABLY AWESOME and KICKING THE BUTT OF LAST CHRISTMAS (which really wouldn't be too hard). Around November 24, I started acquiring foil-wrapped Christmas chocolates, amassing, I'd guess conservatively, a thousand hundred million pounds. We would not, my friend, be short of those ever again!

During the early part of December, my husband and I traded e-mails with links for the toys and gifts we'd be getting for Violet for Hanukkah and Christmas to make up for the poor showing of the previous year (which, by the way, she had not noticed at all). We got not one but two American Girl dolls, several outfits for their galas and tea dances, a horse for them to ride, and bought books and DVDs and Hello Kitty products and a new trundle bed so Violet could have sleepovers.

Paul came home one night from work as I was trying desperately to cram something else—an Olympic-sized swimming pool—into our hall closet. He had bags in his hand, too. We were both shoving coats aside and moving bicycle pumps and basketballs out of the way, when I heard a small voice say, *"Enough."* It was hard to hear, muffled under boxes of a Wii and a Wii Fit and several Wii dance party disks. But I heard it nonetheless. And Paul did, too. We looked at each other and smiled.

"Got a little carried away, I guess," Paul said.

"Yeah," I agreed.

We realized then that we needed to express our feelings of good fortune in some way other than spoiling our kid to smithereens. Some of the booty was donated to Toys for Tots, a charity that gives gifts to needy kids. But I was also preoccupied with finding something else for us to do. In the past, that had meant fostering a dog, but I was in foster jail. Paul (rightly) felt we had too many dogs that were not well behaved and that bringing in another, even temporarily, would cause him to leap out a window. I still trolled my Yahoo! group list and every so often my heart would jump when there was a dog in a Manhattan shelter, because I could at least pull it from the shelter (and kiss it and talk with it) until it went to an open foster home. Truthfully, I was aching to get a foster dog. Violet had been very captivated by a book series called Puppy Place about a family, the Petersons, who fostered puppies. The family consisted of parents Betsy and Paul, and their three kids, Lizzie, Charles, and Adam (whom they called the Bean). In the Puppy Place books, Paul, Charles, Lizzie, and the Bean were the puppy enthusiasts, while the mom was the reluctant one. Oh, she could be reasoned with by the end of the first chapter, but she preferred cats. Violet was kind of smitten with the Lizzie character, and she wanted us to foster, too. Only she wanted to foster Yorkies (Yorkish terriers, as she called them), specifically a female so she could put a pink bow in her hair and name her Princess or Sugar. So she was on board; it was just the Paul in our family who was reluctant, and he was not as easy to influence as Betsy Peterson.

I had been talking with Sheryl, the head of our rescue group, about other things when I innocently asked if there were any dogs coming into foster. She said that, amazingly, there were none at the moment. It was "amazing" because the last time I checked, they were in need of eight foster homes within a two-week period.

"We've got a potential that I'm talking to a vet about—she has a malabsorption problem. The owner can't afford all the tests. There is also some neurological disorder," she said. "But it could be a problem for the group, because she has issues with bowel control. She is, for sure, special needs and young."

"Issues of bowel control?" I asked.

"The owner said she's 'fecally incontinent.'"

"WHOA!" I yelled. "Is that a thing?"

"I'll get more info after I speak to her vet," she said.

I was reeling. I had unhousebroken dogs, but the idea of "fecal incontinence" was blowing my mind. I just imagined this dog walking around with poop streaming behind her . . . behind.

I talked more with Sheryl. I was curious about the poor thing.

"The problem," Sheryl said, "is that she may just be unadoptable. She will most likely be someone's permanent foster and we just don't have room for that at the moment."

Permanent fosters were dogs that for one reason

or another could not be adopted out and so would be kept permanently with one of our foster families, their expenses covered by our group. Some had medical problems, some were too old, and some had behavior problems. It was a lot to ask someone and it also made one less spot for adoptable fosters. Sheryl would speak to the dog's vet and try to get a better picture of the medical situation and then discuss with the board whether this dog would be accepted into rescue or not. It wasn't a life-or-death situation where the dog was about to be homeless.

I asked Sheryl what the owner's letter had said.

The gentleman explained that the dog was three years old, had been in many homes, and was diagnosed with malabsorption syndrome and pancreatitis by a former vet. The dog was on a special diet and pills. But the owner and the vet weren't even sure this was an actual problem. The dog seemed to have neurological issues and "mental" problems. The main thing was that she was fecally incontinent; when she had to go, she would just go, whether you were holding her or she was walking. He also said she was a very sweet girl, very affectionate, good around other dogs, very playful. And he asked that we help her.

"OY!" I cried.

"What is this about?" Sheryl asked. "You're not looking to foster, *are you*?"

"Noooooo," I said, sounding more like yes.

Sheryl laughed her heartiest.

Walking to the train to get Violet, I decided to check in with my friend Nicole. She was an amazing vet, chief of oncology at the Animal Medical Center, one of the top-rated animal hospitals in the country. We both had kids at the same time and would get together to alleviate our guilt. She didn't have to feel bad about feeding her son yellow cake with frosting before dinner, and I didn't have to feel bad about my daughter having her fourth bottle instead of food. Our dog ships were run equally tight.

"What's up?" she answered.

"There's a possible foster dog," I told her.

"Uh-oh."

"I'm not taking her, but the group is trying to decide whether or not she should come in to foster. She has malabsorption syndrome and some neurological thing and she's 'fecally incontinent.'"

"And you don't want her?" Nicole said, chuckling.

"I'm just not ready to be single," I said, imagining Paul's response.

She gave me her opinion, which, as usual with these cases, was that there was some important bit of information missing. Malabsorption is very treatable and doesn't cause fecal incontinence. It sounded like that symptom had to do with the neurological stuff, but there was not enough data here. I told her that Sheryl was going to speak to the dog's vet and she told me what to have Sheryl ask, and then ended up deciding she'd call the vet herself.

"Oh, you are the *best*!" I was so relieved, because she'd asked me to see what I could find out about the rectal exam.

I have to be honest here. I am a person who is very grossed out by bodily functions. And I don't like to discuss anything in the neighborhood of the butt. There was a dog I was thinking of fostering several years ago that had some sort of problem where his anus was either missing or in the wrong place. He needed surgery, and I was just so unbelievably relieved when someone said he was too far from me and he went somewhere else. I know some people who love to discuss these things; my dad's mother was obsessed. That's just not me. And yet I spend a good portion of my waking hours picking up canine feces in my house or on my dog walks. That doesn't bother me . . . which is supremely fortunate.

Nicole talked to the vet and said their office was also a bit in the dark. They hadn't been able to do a full evaluation because the guy couldn't afford the tests. But the vet said she was a very, very sweet girl and would make a terrific dog for someone. She admitted that she had even considered taking her herself.

"Hmm," I said. "So it might be fixable?"

"It might be," Nicole said.

"Or it might not," I said.

"Right."

"The guy who has her also said there was something mentally wrong with her."

Nicole laughed. "She sounds like a lemon dog, and you know how I feel about lemons."

I did; Nicole loved the lemon dogs.

"If she's dumb, that's even better," Nicole said. "Smart dogs are so much harder. Who needs it?"

I told Sheryl what Nicole said, and asked her what the dog's name was.

"Winnie," Sheryl replied.

"Winnie?" I repeated. "Winnie as in Winnie the Pooh-per?"

Sheryl laughed. "You can call her anything you like, just not one of your crazy flower names."

"Me? What am I naming her for?"

Sheryl took a long breath. "Then why are you so interested in her?"

"Okay," I said, "maybe I am."

"At this time, Julie, I think there are only two choices for us to make. One, yes, she would probably be a permanent foster, and she's only three years old, so that could last a very long time. Who knows if the fecal incontinence will ever improve. From what this fellow said, she has no control over it and will 'go' even if you are holding her. It's a huge commitment. Probably diapers would help at least to contain it. We could get an MRI if Nicole and the neurologist think it might reveal something. An X-ray to see if there's a cyst? All her other problems can be lived with, but the fecal incontinence is a huge decision that you and Paul would have to consider."

"Or?" I asked.

"We would have to let him know that we cannot take her because she would be a permanent foster and we don't have a home like that available. His explanation for surrendering her is lack of time and finances." He had only had her for three months.

I made a lot of *uggh* and *blurgh* noises. "Okay. What about this . . . I really, really do want to take her, because she's been in several homes and my heart is breaking about her being dumped again." I continued, "The problem for me . . . us . . . is the permanence, but I think that I can get her adopted. I would like to take her and get her a ton of excellent medical attention. I would cover all of the costs of the tests, foster her, and then try and place her. The problem comes if I can't, but I think I can. So the 'if I can't find a home for her' is the issue right now."

"I have no more cautions," Sheryl said. "If you can deal with Winnie the Pooper and her difficulties, I'm thrilled and touched by your concern for her."

"Don't say that."

Sheryl laughed.

I took a deep breath. "So, what do you think?"

Sheryl paused and said, "I think you are a chump. But I love you anyway!"

More than the problem of the incontinence, I was worried about my dogs beating up on this sweet girl. They were incredibly aggressive with other dogs on the streets and were even worse to ones that dared come near our apartment. Thus began my fretting.

My head was in a permanent loop—must take dog, my dogs bad, shouldn't take dog, dog doesn't get rescued, must take dog, etc. . . . I picked Violet up from school and we were going to meet Paul at a diner. I was somewhat quiet, but no one noticed.

"You might notice I'm being quiet," I said. "Wanna know what I'm thinking about?"

Paul looked at me. "No."

I raised my eyebrows.

"You're thinking about that crapping dog, right?"

"I know we can't take her."

"This is where I'm supposed to say, 'Sure, let's take her!'" Paul said. "But I'm not going to."

"I know, I know."

I understood his reluctance, because I felt it, too. I also worried that the dog would have nowhere to go. And I felt that she had not yet had a proper diagnosis, which I knew I could get her. Nicole was going to talk to the neurologists at the Animal Medical Center and she had a good general vet there for me to see. What if this supposed fecal incontinence was a simple problem? Maybe she had worms or something.

Paul spoke. "If it was really temporary—a foster situation—I'd consider it."

"Well, that's what we're assuming it is," I said.

"But what if no one wants to adopt her?"

"That would be a chance we'd be taking no matter what dog we fostered."

I started "what-iffing." There was a woman in the rescue group, Carolyn, who had a kennel and training facility, and she'd taken a couple of permanent fosters. What if Carolyn agreed to take this dog if no one adopted her or she wasn't working out with our crew? Paul thought for a minute and said if we had a backup like that, he'd agree. I called Sheryl right then and asked if she could talk to Carolyn. Also, when she spoke to her, could she see whether she had any ideas on how to keep my dogs from abusing this potential foster.

The next day I spoke to Carolyn on the phone. She

said that yes, if the dogs didn't get along with her, she'd take Winnie, even if it meant keeping her. She was unflinching. She asked me about my dogs and when I told her, she started talking to me about having to be the leader of my pack. I said I wasn't the leader of my pack. Wisteria was, or sometimes Beatrice.

"JULIE!" she said, like she'd known me my whole life.

"I know, I know," I said. "I'm not exactly a trainer, and they are really tough."

"We have a training boot camp here, and one of the things we teach—"

"Stop!" I said. "You have a training boot camp? Can I send Fiorello and Wisteria, my problem children, there? Seriously." There was no point in sending Bea, she was housebroken.

"Sure," she said. "We run a tight ship, though. They are going to be housebroken as well as leash trained."

"Woo-hoo!" I said.

"In fact, if you want, we'll pick up the foster, and you can come get her here and drop off your two."

"How long would it be?" I asked.

"Usually just about a week or two," Carolyn said, "depending on the dogs."

It was shaping up to be a plan. I came into the living room and told Paul.

A wide grin spread across his face. "That could be my Christmas present."

So now there was something in it for everyone. Paul could get housebroken, well-trained dogs, the rescue dog could come into foster, and I could live up to my chump name. It wasn't going to work before Christmas, so we made arrangements for New Year's Eve.

"What should we call her?" I asked.

This was always a special time in our household: the choosing of a name for a dog. We had this flower theme going, which of course began with naming our daughter Violet. Then we named our senior foster dog Dahlia and her puppies Wisteria and Fiorello ("little flower" in Italian), but Paul felt that a flower name for this foster would mean we were keeping her. So we came up with Clementine, a sweet Christmastime fruit, and also the name of an old French bulldog in our former neighborhood who had such serious neurological issues that she walked in endless circles; Paul and I loved her and wanted to adopt her, but there was a small problem in that she wasn't up for adoption.

I told Sheryl we would take her.

"I'm stunned!" she said, her voice dripping with sarcasm. "What's the name? Hydrangea?"

"Clementine," I reported.

"Clementine?" she said, sighing. "Jules, most people name their dogs with two syllables and end it with *ee*, so it kind of rolls off the tongue. Tilly, Sydney, Riggsie, Wally, Kelly, Nedley, Fizzy"—all her dogs' names. "But *Clementine?* I meant to discuss that with you when you came up with Fiorello."

"Fiorello has meaning—it's Italian for 'He Who Cannot Be Trained,'" I said. "And we're planning to call her Clemmie."

"Oh," she said. "Clemmie. I like that."

I e-mailed another group member, Joy, who was my friend and foster adviser. She had taken a zillion special-needs dogs, including a deaf terror named Beadoe, and various others with far-ranging health issues. She had even taken the dog with a broken behind.

"Did you hear about the foster I'm getting?"

"Girl, you got a good heart," she wrote. "I wouldn't have gone anywhere near her."

This sentiment was being echoed by many. When I told my mother I was taking her, she said, "You're kidding, right?"

"Nope," I said finally.

Why? Why would I take her? I didn't have to. And yet I felt like I did. This person was going to give her up, and if our group didn't take her, I didn't know what this owner would do with her. And no one in the group could take her at this time. I just kept thinking that if she'd been my dog and became fecally incontinent, I'd work something out. I knew it would be some kind of challenge, but that's kind of why I did rescue. It was always nice to get a great little dog who was easy to adopt out, but the special ones—the old ones, the sick ones, the blind and deaf ones, the *pregnant* ones—they really needed someone to help them.

We made arrangements and I started feeling a tiny bit guilty about the boot camp. I talked to Ann, who swore that dogs are happier when they are trained and know what they're supposed to do. So I told myself this was just like when Violet didn't want to go to pre-kindergarten and I made her do it, despite how incredibly painful it was for all of us.

On New Year's Eve morning I rented a car and we drove out to Carolyn's in New Jersey with Fiorello and Wisteria, and since Beatrice loves a car ride, we took her, too. I had packed two weeks' worth of food and their halters and leashes, and that was it. Violet was very worried about leaving them, but she understood that if we were going to live this Puppy Place book, we had to go through with it. Also, if the dogs were trained, we'd be able to foster again in the future.

Kamp Kanine was located in Little Falls, New Jersey. An editor friend who'd boarded her dogs there told me it wasn't much to look at, but it was Disney World for dogs. We parked and leaped over enormous heaps of snow to get to the door. It was a nice place, with Christmas cookies on the counter and a scented candle burning in the reception area (the scent, I believe, was called "Unsmelly Dog").

Carolyn and one of her workers came out to greet us. I was relieved to not be worrying about how the dogs behaved. It was like bringing a sick person to a doctor: it was okay if they sneezed. And though my dogs didn't sneeze, they did both take dumps on the floor.

"Oh no, I'm sorry!" I said, fishing in my pocket for a bag.

The worker swept in with paper towels and a spray. "Are you kidding? This is all we do," she said, happily eradicating the mess.

I gave their leashes to Carolyn, and someone brought Clemmie out. She was painfully thin, you could see her bones, and she was skating all over the floor with her little floppy paws. My dogs tried to attack her in a further demonstration of their need for boot camp. Carolyn pulled them back and said, "No!" I was impressed.

"Do you want to say good-bye before I take them back?" she asked.

"No." I didn't want any dramatic departures, just git 'em outta here and let us go.

We didn't discuss what we interpreted "fecally incontinent" to mean, but Paul and I were both under the impression that aside from that, her bathroom habits were impeccable. We had pictured her trotting outside to do her pees in the park. If you thought that too, well, then we were both wrong.

If Paul and I died at the same moment—in some dog pee–related death, slipping in a puddle and cracking our heads open—and were buried together, the joint gravestone would read, "They never learned." They *never* learned.

We dropped Fiorello and Wisteria off at boot camp with the best intentions. Clementine would come to our apartment, she'd stay in her little heavily lined playpen, and she could be as fecally incontinent as she needed to be. No trouble for anyone. As far as we could tell, we'd dealt with far worse in much stupider ways. When I got home I set about putting together the playpen. The whole thing was a mass of plastic sticks that you fit together like Legos—very user-friendly after you figure out which side is up, which for some reason took me about eleven tries. But then there was this little door that came with a bag of seven thousand metal hinges and bolts and two kinds of screws and pages of directions in nine languages. I put it aside and left it for Paul.

I watched Clementine walk around our house, waiting for something to happen. I'd bought an eighteen-roller of paper towels and a gallon of cleaner. Every time she took a step or walked into a new room, Violet and I raced to watch her, like she was about to lay a golden egg or something. You can imagine my surprise and delight when she didn't seem to be pooping at all. Her back legs, which I had been told dragged, didn't drag all that much. When she walked, it seemed like she was wearing big, fluffy bedroom slippers on her back feet or needed to have her pants hemmed. Compared with what I imagined she'd be like, what we had come home with was A-plus-plus.

New Year's Eve had started, and Beatrice was going nuts with the horns and the shouting and the loud music, but Clemmie was fine. With Fiorello and Wisteria at boot camp, our apartment felt like a rest home. It was quiet. I took Clemmie and Beatrice for a walk, and no one pulled my arms out of the sockets. Clemmie actually pooped outside—granted, it just sort of fell out, she didn't actually squat—but still, she was seemingly far less fecally incontinent than our perfectly healthy dogs who were at boot camp. We came in, and Clemmie got in her bed. We'd taken it out of her pen, because Violet was now using the area as a drawing studio and it was just too crowded. Clemmie was lying in her bed with her little face all mashed up and oh! Was she missing her family? Was she scared? She was so so so so so so cute! Paul took a picture of her. I e-mailed it to her former owner, and he wrote back, "Don't be surprised if she tries to get under the covers!"

I said to Paul, "Clemmie sleeps with them?"

And he said, "Well, we'd still be down one dog in the bed . . ."

And there you are reading this and thinking, *Oh, Julie, you didn't let the fecally incontinent foster dog in your bed on New Year's Eve, did you?* And I say, "Well, yes, but GOOD NEWS, she didn't *poop* in the bed!"

Paul stayed on the couch with Bea, who'd been going crazy all night. (For some reason sleeping on the couch with him helps her.) In the predawn hours when Paul came back in our room to go to bed, he found an unfortunate puddle of pee on his side of the bed. What could we say? She tricked us! I was crabby all morning, but I had to stop my complaining when I realized that I had most definitely gotten up on the right side of the bed.

Anyway, we'd get that little hingey door put up on the pen as soon as we could.

Some other things about Clemmie that I quickly

found out: She was *starving*. Yes, she was thin, but she was also crazed about eating. Carolyn and I had puzzled over the fact that she came with this big bag of low-fat prescription food and a small scoop that she'd been getting twice a day. I had to wonder if maybe they were underfeeding her to keep her from pooping. Whatever it was, I gave her a lot more food than she'd been getting, which she gobbled up as it was hitting the bowl.

My dogs were very leisurely about their food, they'd eat it over the course of the evening, but that wouldn't happen with Vacuum-Lips around. I had to keep picking up Bea's food every time she left the kitchen.

And Winnie did poop in the house. But at least they were neat and dry and easy to pick up.

She also was not fond of her little pen with the functioning door. We talked about getting a crate for her (which the previous owner said he'd used, but she cried in it) but it seemed like if she was going to be "going," it would be better to give her an area with newspaper rather than a small box that she couldn't move around in. I didn't want her sleeping in her own mess. We put her bed and blanket and toys in the pen, and some newspaper and a bowl of water, because she was so thirsty all the time. I turned out the lights and listened to her cry. Sheryl's "you're a chump, but I love you" echoed through my head . . . mostly the chump part. I went into my bedroom and read and tried hard not to hear the whimpers. It was sleep training all over again. I wondered if I should sit by the pen and move away a little more every night—ferberize Clemmie. The next day we'd be seeing the vet. I'd get Clemmie healthy and well and adopted. I was determined.

At eight-thirty a.m., we were heading over to the Animal Medical Center on the East Side. I wrapped Clemmie in a towel (just in case she had an accident) and hailed a cab. I put her on my lap and she sat up and looked out the window. I was staring at the back of her head, moving left to right watching nail salons and gourmet food stores and yogurt shops go by.

"There used to be an amazing ice cream parlor here called Agora that my dad took us to when we were kids," I said to her quietly. "And this is where Maxwell's

Plum was. A New York fixture. My aunt Alex took me there in the eighties, and my fruit salad had star-shaped kiwis and tiny scoops of sorbet. I was so sad when it closed." The cab driver looked at me in the rearview mirror. *Mind your business,* I thought. *I can talk to the dog if I want.*

I hadn't really had time alone with Clemmie. Beatrice was a little snippy with her, so she kept her distance from me at home, but here in the taxi I felt her vulnerability. She was a stranger in a strange land, and it had to be so hard. I kissed the top of her head and she turned around and licked my cheek one time.

We got to the Animal Medical Center without incident (or an accident in the cab). Our vet was sweet and young, very smart and sympathetic to my plight. She gave Clemmie an exam, talking to her in a cute puppy voice, and then brought her to the neurologists to be checked out. They could see indications of something, but they felt strongly that whatever was wrong was an anatomical abnormality and it wasn't likely anything could be done about it. For that reason, they didn't recommend an MRI, but did suggest giving her Prilosec, which I knew of as a heartburn drug. A more seasoned medical mind might have dug deeper into this, but when I hear clinical jargon, my mind goes into a fuzzy state. The words simply went over my head. At that moment, I fixed on the notion that she had something wrong with her that couldn't be corrected but could be managed. I think I loved her so much I wanted it to be okay, and figured there would be a kind and tolerant home she could go to. Maybe somewhere without a lot of rugs.

More than the neurological stuff, I was wondering what the deal was with the pancreatitis and malabsorption issues, which were likely addressable. She needed a fasting blood test for diagnosis, which was not going to be easy, since the girl didn't miss a meal! (The vet tech was giving her treats while we were there, one after another. "You're so skinny and hungry!" she kept telling Clemmie, who already knew.) I figured by the following week she'd be less voracious, so we scheduled her blood test for then. We also were given a urine sample kit for her. I told the vet that thus far the urine had been hard to catch, as most of it was in my rug (and Paul's side of the bed). She gave me a little suction thing to suck it off the floor. I was happy that night when I saw her puddle on the bathroom floor, which was easier to retrieve than from the wool carpet. Violet watched me as I syringed it up and put in the vial.

"Can I do that?" she asked.

"It's pee!" I said.

"Oh! I never get to do anything fun," she groused. It was true; I was a very selfish mother when it came to picking up various dog eliminations. I made a point to really look into my dark heart and see what was driving me to deprive her.

So as much as I hate the bodily function topic, it became my life. I ended up picking up a LOT of waste from Clemmie (once she started eating more, her, ahem, output increased) and really, I didn't mind. Okay, I admit that when I saw it on the carpet and not the wood floor it did bum me out, but Fiorello and Wisteria have inured me to the shock. The doctor suggested a low-residue food, so it was easier to pick up. And thus far, I was not at all convinced that she was fecally incontinent. She went over and over in about the same places, which meant she was aware enough to go to those spots (on my lovely yellow rug from India, for example). Once she began going, she didn't have control, as evidenced by the wide area that it fell in (think Stonehenge or Easter Island), which we called her "crap circles." But if that was grass instead of our rugs, then she'd be fine. Now I started to wonder about the existence of a patient, kindhearted person with a doggie door and a fenced-in yard.

By about the fourth day she was looking less skeletal, which was not surprising because she was consuming her food, and most likely Bea's food, at a Kobayashi-like rate. When she wasn't eating, she would lie on the floor with a small stuffed Boston terrier that came with her. Sometimes she'd nuzzle it, other times she'd chew it, always she'd sleep with it. I was knocked out by the cuteness of it and found myself taking her picture all day long.

I'd not given much thought to what her personality would be, and it took me some time to notice just how endearing her mannerisms were. Because I was so keen on watching her backside, I was missing what the front was doing (other than eating). She was very much a heartbreaker. She was sweet with everyone, and occasionally she'd just go off on her own and burrow into her stuffed doggie, like it was her coping mechanism for being in yet another new place. She didn't have a mean bone in her body and she was extremely pretty—large, soft eyes, a cute muzzle, a good degree of flatness in the face, nice ears. Her markings were good, and her chest looked like a black-and-white cookie. And with the little "shuffle off to Buffalo" walk, she was just adorable.

We got fairly regular reports on the progress of the dream team from Kamp Kanine. It seemed that Fiorello wanted nothing more than to be held by various employees and Wisteria was the class bully. Carolyn would not give us a return date yet; it was still in the neighborhood of a week or two. But looking more like "or two."

Violet and I brought Clemmie to the vet for her fasting blood test. We sat in the examining room waiting for the doctor. There was a poster on the wall of "dog poisons," a picture of a cartoon puppy in the center of chocolate kisses, cupcakes, grapes, onions, and garlic—all the things that dogs should not eat. Violet asked me to take her picture in front of it (because it had a picture of a dog and cupcakes). The doctor came in as she was posing.

"How is Clementine doing?" she asked, immediately impressed with how much weight she'd gained.

"Pretty good!" I said. "I don't think she's incontinent."

"That's great!"

"I mean, she goes in the same place most of the time, so that seems like not-incontinence, right?"

"Maybe," the vet said hopefully.

A few days later the blood test came back perfect. There was nothing wrong with either her pancreas or her digestion. There was bacteria in her urine, though, so we needed to bring her back in for a sterile urine test where they take it right from her body.

"Yeah, that urine sample came off my bathroom floor," I said. "The bacteria is most likely ours."

After a new urine test, everything was confirmed to be excellent. She got a clean bill of health, except she shuffled when she walked.

I e-mailed Sheryl and Carolyn. We all discussed the fact that we almost didn't take this dog, and what a relief to know that everything seemed to be okay. Violet began writing a Petfinder ad for Clemmie; she was now adoptable.

Later that week, Violet had a doctor's appointment in which she needed to get blood taken. She was very upset about it, because a couple of years earlier she had had a really bad experience; the blood draw had been botched and it was pretty traumatic for her. I did not sleep the night before as I tossed around thinking of ways out of the test. Maybe while the nurse wasn't looking I could stick my arm into Violet's sleeve and get the needle in my arm instead of hers. I mean, I was her mother, our blood had to be somewhat similar, right? The appointment turned out fine, but it took a very long time, and when we got home, we found that Clemmie had gone on the rug. Violet stared at the oddly shaped poop circle.

"Mom," she said thoughtfully, "I think Clemmie pooped in the shape of a heart because she felt sad for me that I had to get my blood taken."

I told this to Paul, who later referred to it as "when Clementine crapped out a sympathy card to Violet."

Now we were nearing four weeks of Fiorello and Wisteria in boot camp. Paul wondered if they were stalling because they'd broken the dogs, but we'd gotten a couple of videos of them (if it really was them—these dogs were well-behaved!). I had mixed feelings about it, worrying first that they'd be mad at me, and then that I'd ruin them again. Carolyn said Wisteria was doing great, that she was turning out to be a real pillar of the Kamp Kanine Kommunity. In the photos she sent of the playroom, Wisteria was a blur, running with tail wagging, and Fiorello was sitting on the sidelines. I could see him thinking, *Has anyone heard from my lawyer about my appeal?*

Finally, we really missed our dogs and wanted them back. Carolyn wanted to bring them to us so she could give us a quick lesson in walking them. On the day of their return, I was nervous waiting in front of the building for them to arrive. I saw Mark, Carolyn's partner and trainer, coming down the block with them. They weren't pulling at all, they were walking, and stopped to sit and heel. When they saw me, they looked at Mark for the okay to say hello. I was crazed, kissing them and screaming, and I felt like a mom whose kids have returned from military school. They were being soldierly and all I could say was, "Look how big you've gotten!"

Mark showed me how to walk them, and then we came upstairs for the true test. I knew my dogs' behavior. Upon finding a strange dog in our home, they would go ballistic. We opened the door, and Clemmie and Bea came up. Fiorello and Wisteria politely said hello and walked around sniffing. I was in shock. SHOCK! Who were these Stepford dogs? What had they done with my baby monsters!

Of course, I was thrilled. This meant that we could walk around the neighborhood and pass dogs on the street without creating a major scene. I would stop being the walking sight gag!

"They're housebroken now!" Carolyn said, sort of threatening me to keep it up. I shook my head in disbelief. They went over the schedule and rules with me. Mark had me walk Wisteria and make her sit. I walked her around and said, "Sit?" (two syllables, the second going way up high).

"It's a command," Mark insisted, "not a request."

I tried again. I did everything wrong, I needed a lot of practice . . . or boot camp.

They both looked at me skeptically as they put their coats on.

"I'm really going to do it!" I said convincingly.

When they left, Wisteria climbed up on the couch and went into a deep sleep. Fiorello stared up at me hard.

"I had to," I told him. "It wasn't personal."

He turned on his heel and walked away from me. A few minutes later that inimitable smell permeated the air. He had ceremoniously taken a dump right in his old spot as if to say, *"I got your boot camp right here."*

Later Carolyn texted me and asked me how they were doing. I told her about Fiorello.

"OH!!" she wrote. "HE'S SO FRESH!"

Clemmie's Petfinder ad was done. We had a wide variety of adorable pictures to choose from, and everyone who saw her thought she was a doll. We had a couple of near misses, and I remembered how long it could take to find a home. That was fine; we could certainly keep her as long as we needed to.

We now had the pleasure of four dogs again and I remembered how that could be. "Very active" is how I saw it; I think Paul thought, "Utter hell."

Though their leash abilities had improved monumentally and permanently, the puppies' housebreaking unraveled in minutes. I believe they had a secret meeting with Clementine à la *Ocean's Eleven* in which they broke the apartment into sectors that each would be responsible for turning into their personal commode. Clemmie took the living room, Wisteria took the dining room, and Fiorello was in charge of halls and bathrooms. I in turn would do my Tour of Doody, eradicating their hard work and requiring them to refocus their dogpower.

Violet had written Clementine's ad:

Hi. I am Clementine. I am a three-year-old Boston terrier, I am NOT housebroken. I AM sweet, good with kids, and dogs. I could be housebroken very easily, all I need is a nice yard. I was a rescue pup. My full name is Clementine Eve Bows. Clementine because I am very sweet and small, Eve because I came to my foster home on New Year's Eve, and Bows because my youngest owner loves Hello Kitty (because Hello Kitty has a bow). I hope you will adopt me so I can play with you, lick your face, and you can train me and love me, and more! Love, Clementine Eve Bows!

I was trying to think more creatively about how to place her. I asked a professional photographer to take a picture of Clemmie. While snapping away he remarked, "She's cute. Is she supposed to be that fat?"

Fat? Oh. My. God. Clemmie went from skin and bones to being a tub without my realizing it. I looked at her the way my mother looked at me when I came home from freshman year: *Oops!*

I posted on Facebook and Tweeted about finding a good "furever" home for Clementine. I had begun to sort of resign myself to having Clemmie with us for a long time when a writer friend, Allison, saw her Petfinder ad on my Twitter feed and wrote to me, "I will take that dog . . . I just melted." I told her to stop joking and she said she wasn't, she'd just asked her husband and he agreed.

It was "just like that"—the perfect home with the perfect person presented itself. Until it was really done, I reserved celebrating, but I was so very happy for both of them. Only when I started filling out the paperwork for her adoption did I realize how much I loved and would miss this little special-needs gal. When people asked me how I could foster and not get attached to the dogs, I'd tell them how I eat extra spinach for the iron I need to harden my heart. And sometimes I can. And sometimes they get in anyway.

It had been a draining experience, and I was looking forward to things calming down a bit when she left us. I made it be known that I was definitely not going to be in foster rotation for a while.

Paul and I also started talking about moving. We loved our apartment, but the neighborhood was a constant trial, and we were finally prepared for it. I did worry about finding a place that would allow us to have all of our dogs. There was a lot of leniency in our building, since as annoying as our dogs were, they weren't selling drugs, which wasn't the case with some of the other tenants.

On a blessedly springlike morning in February, I took the four dogs out. Some friends were filming a television show on the first floor and just outside of the building, and I stopped to say hello and meet some of the actors. Everyone was impressed by my dogs' behavior, which was a coup in itself (thank you, Kamp Kanine). There was a little whispering, and I thought they were going to ask us to be in the show. I was smoothing down my bedhead in preparation.

"What?" I said to my friend Robin, who'd brought her own dog, Silencio, to the set.

"Oh," she said sheepishly. "I was just asking Jane if you'd seen the pages describing your building."

I laughed. "No, but now you have to show me."

"I told you she won't be offended," Jane said.

It said something like "To put it mildly, this is not Park Avenue." I feigned insult and slipped in that we were planning to move . . . not to Park Avenue. Unless it was a very dog-friendly building.

A few years before, I'd had a very special foster dog. He'd come from a Pennsylvania family who had previously surrendered a bunch of dogs that ended up all being kept by their foster families. They were just that wonderful. In the group they became known as "the PA Dogs." My PA dog wasn't like the rest of them; he was scared and fragile. I named him Moses and he became a dog of my heart, the love of my dog life. Very tragically and suddenly, he was hit by a car and killed while I stood helplessly by. I had always felt that I had not had enough time with my Mosie. Every so often I'd e-mail Jane, our intake coordinator, and Joy, who had Moses' brother, Cal, and ask if they'd heard from the PA people. I knew that though our group had taken five or so of their dogs, they had more and there was a chance those would be coming our way.

While my friend's application for Clementine was being processed, I got an e-mail from Jane. The subject line was PA DOGS. She'd heard from the guy. His girlfriend had left him with their small child and four dogs and he needed to surrender three of them. One was Moses' mother, Sparkira, and the other two were his littermate sister Sasha and a brother from the litter after, Buddy. She knew I had a full house and was about to go on foster hiatus, but she had to let me know, just in case.

"I'll take one," I wrote back immediately. I told Paul and he understood. Thank God there was a home waiting for Clemmie, but if there hadn't been, well then, we would've dealt with having five dogs. There was just no way I was not going to do this. Just fostering one, of course.

I debated taking Sasha, Moses' actual littermate, but I'd had a little difficulty with both Beatrice and Wisteria being tough girls to Clemmie, who was entirely submissive. She got bullied and immediately lay down on her back. Another female might not do that. When I'd talked to training friends, they'd agreed that a boy might work better, so I requested Buddy. Sasha would go to a member in New Jersey and Sparkira would go to someone on Long Island.

I had a strong feeling about this, that sense that it was meant to be. I had a visceral need to get this dog. Moses' death had been such a tragedy. One of the feelings I'd had when I saw him die was that I desperately wanted to turn back time and have him again. When I'd heard about the new batch of PA dogs, a part of me thought, *I'm getting Moses back!* I had to continually tell myself that this wasn't Moses any more than I was my brother. But still there was some connection. He was Moses' brother and he was in need. That was enough.

We had set the plans for the weekend. Allison and her husband were picking up Clemmie at noon on Sunday and Buddy (who we were debating calling Huck, Hickory, or Zeke like the Scarecrow, Tin Man, and Lion from *The Wizard of Oz*) was due to arrive later that day. It was not the ideal plan, one out, one in, but it was just how it was working out.

On the rainy Friday morning while transportation arrangements were being made, I got an e-mail from Sheryl. Sasha, Moses' sister who was being fostered in New Jersey, had passed away. It appeared to have been cancer. This news stunned me.

At 12:05 p.m. on Sunday, Allison and her husband, Dave, buzzed from downstairs at the exact moment my cell phone rang. It was Melissa from Northeast Boston Terrier Rescue, who was bringing Buddy. They were on the George Washington Bridge just minutes from our home.

"Oh, goody," Paul muttered. As I'd imagined, there would be a five-dog layover. I started to circle.

Clemmie's bag was packed. Allison and Dave rang the doorbell and came in. Allison's face broke into a wide grin and she kept looking at her husband with a "You see? What did I tell you?!" expression. He sat down and Clemmie came right up to him.

"You are not going to lick me," Dave said. "Not going to happen." He was petting her and she was leaping up at him on her floppy legs, her tongue outstretched. On the third try, she won, and he smiled, defeated by the signature Clementine charm.

The buzzer rang again, and this time it was Melissa. I suddenly realized how nervous and excited I was about meeting Buddy. I went out into the hall by myself so I could greet him alone before he met the throngs. I stood and waited for the elevator for a long while and then I saw a blond head bobbing up the stairs; Melissa had decided to walk the nine flights! I caught sight of Buddy; he was tired! And as he got closer, I began to recognize his little Mosie-like square head. I felt overcome with emotion as he strolled over to me; there were a lot of similarities. Aside from his head, his muzzle had the same shape and spots. God, he was adorable!

He wasn't frightened, though he was certainly wondering where he was, and I picked him up. He felt like Moses, but of course he wasn't Moses. In under a minute, I'd fallen in love with him.

The dogs all met and growled and barked, hackles going up, and then finally settled down. Allison and Dave took Clementine and said good-bye. I put on the halter I'd gotten her when she'd first arrived, and not surprisingly I had to loosen it . . . a lot. Melissa left too and we sat around with the dogs, letting everyone get comfortable. Again I had to thank Kamp Kanine because Wisteria and Fiorello were really sweet and welcoming. (Beatrice, not so much.) We gave the dogs some treats and dispersed. I sat down at my desk and Buddy looked up at me. I smiled at those familiar eyes. I picked him up so he could snooze on my lap, which he did. The weight felt so good. I picked up the phone and called my mother, who'd been eager to hear about Clemmie's departure and Buddy's arrival.

"Well," I said, "good news! We're down to four dogs!" Buddy let out a contented snort.

"You aren't planning on keeping him, are you?" my mom asked.

I scratched behind Buddy's ear. "No," I said to her, but to him I nodded yes.

And we thought that everyone would live happily ever after. Unfortunately, like most dog stories, this one, while filled with joy, also had its share of sorrow.

After Clementine settled in with Allison and Dave, she had some really good housebreaking days and seemed to be doing quite well. I was so happy that I had been right. Except I wasn't right. It was clear that her neurological condition was more than slight; she had responded well to training, but she was still having way too many accidents. Her shuffling walk had progressed into more serious balance issues, and her anxiety started to rise. Allison's vet recommended taking her to a veterinary neurologist. After a series of expensive and difficult tests, the condition was pinpointed. She had a Chiari malformation, which is a degenerative neurological condition. With the possibility that things would only get worse, the amount of daily care she would require, and the options for treating her (brain surgery for one), it was clearly not manageable for Allison and Dave to keep her. This was not a simple decision for them, as they were totally in love with her.

I forwarded her test results to Nicole, who was on vacation in Florida. Being a veterinary oncologist, Nicole spent much of her time discussing options for very sick pets. She thought, given the way things were going, Clemmie didn't have a lot of time left, but it didn't seem like she was in pain at the moment. She was still eating and drinking and playing and barking.

Allison and I decided that Clementine would come back to my home, where she had seemed happy and comfortable, to live out her final days. As much as it broke Allison's and Dave's hearts to give her up, they knew this would be best for Clemmie. I knew it, too, even though it meant that for however long it was, we'd have five dogs. I could have brought Clemmie to Carolyn's, but it was no longer an option personally. I told Violet she was coming back to us because she was very ill. She explained it to my mom that Clemmie needed to come back to our house because she knew us better. Almost daily she explained to Clemmie about the nice things they have in heaven.

Allison and I had a long talk after Clemmie was returned. I think we both felt that we'd let her down. Then we realized that if I hadn't taken her, she would have been dumped in a shelter. And she was so cute she would have been adopted out and most likely discarded again. Allison's getting her diagnosed prevented her from being re-homed further. Together we had broken the cycle of her being bounced around. Somehow that gave us solace.

And so now Paul and Violet and I do whatever we can to make sure Clemmie is comfortable and safe and, okay, a little bit spoiled. And though I dread the inevitable, I feel lucky for every day that I'm still able to see her sweet face.

3.

There Is a Dog House
in New Orleans

On the morning of August 28, 2005, I was looking
at my eyes in the bathroom mirror. It was my
daughter Violet's second birthday and I was blowing up
pale pink mouse-shaped balloons for her Angelina Bal-
lerina birthday party. The process of trying to get the air
into the mouse's ears had given me cause to believe I
might have blown out an eyeball. I wanted to check and
make sure my eyeballs were still in place. In fact, they
were, so I went back to work.

I was a little anxious. We'd been to some other two-
year-olds' birthday parties, and there'd been catering,

pony rides, clowns who brought elaborate craft projects, actors dressed up as Disney characters who led Tony-worthy sing-alongs. The goody bags were frequently more impressive than my wedding gifts.

Our party was different. I made three types of sand-wiches and a cake that Paul decorated with a pirouet-ting Angelina made from pink and purple frosting. We had a pin-the-tail-on-the-donkey game, a piñata (with strings, no beating), and some other "retro" games. It really came down to the fact that these kids were two and under, they didn't have their party-judging chops yet, and if it stunk, they wouldn't even know.

It didn't. It turned out to be one of the best parties ever. Well, maybe not that, but no one bled or cried, and that worked for me. It was also exhausting. When it was over, Paul and I were bringing bags of garbage into our hallway. We saw our Italian neighbor, Umberto. "Have you seen the television?" he asked, covering his mouth. "Those poor people in New Orleans."

I had no idea what he was talking about.

. . .

That morning, while I was twisting Happy Birthday streamers from window to wall, the mayor of New Orleans was ordering the first-ever mandatory evacuation of New Orleans. Hurricane Katrina was on a direct path for the city. When my neighbor told me about it, the hurricane had already struck and the levees broke and the city was under water. Then I read about it in *The New York Times* and watched footage on CNN. I didn't have friends or relatives in Louisiana, I'd never been there, but I remember thinking, *How could this be happening in the United States?* I'd been in New York City on 9/11 and certainly wondered how that could've occurred, but this was somehow different.

It wasn't until years later that I understood the depth of the tragedy of what had happened in New Orleans.

Five years after Katrina, Paul and I talked about taking a little trip. I'd spent much of the time we were broke fantasizing about lying on a white beach by a turquoise ocean drinking something rummy out of a coconut, but when it came down to it, it wasn't really a "Paul and Julie" kind of trip. One of the medications Paul took made him very sensitive to the sun—he was like a little gefilte fish, but he never seemed to remember that fact until the end of the afternoon when we were discussing what constituted a third-degree burn.

So when I was invited to participate in a fund-raiser for animals at a bookstore in New Orleans, it seemed like a perfect opportunity to travel. I'd been itching to go there for a long time, and now had friends who were involved in animal rescue there and I was really curious about it. My friend Ken, who lived there and rescued pit bulls, told me people took vacations to New Orleans just to volunteer. It was a whole industry called "voluntourism."

"Well, I'm not doing that!" I said.

This was a vacation. I wanted to eat the huge buffet breakfast, and not walk dogs or make school lunches. I wanted to stretch out in a big bed and look at art galleries and go see movies. I didn't want to "voluntour," I wanted to "pay-to-relax." Four days didn't seem like an excessive amount of time to do that.

I e-mailed a virtual friend, Laura, who was living in California when Katrina hit, and had dropped everything to fly to New Orleans and rescue abandoned animals. She was part of the Stealth Volunteers; I wanted to meet her and hear about what she'd done. I have always been fascinated by real-life heroic types. I e-mailed her about meeting for dinner to talk about rescue during Katrina and asked her about the group she currently worked with, Animal Rescue New Orleans (ARNO), and the situation post-Katrina. She wrote back:

> *It will be nice to have you here. Animal Rescue*
> *New Orleans is the local no-kill shelter and they*
> *are still pulling animals off the streets. Good news*
> *is that the numbers have dwindled . . . though we*
> *still pull dogs that are feral off of the street. That*
> *phenomenon occurred quite often here after*
> *Katrina. Street dogs that had never had much*

*human contact became feral very quickly . . .
normally it takes many generations for dogs to
"go feral" (as opposed to cats who can "go feral"
in two generations) but because of the conditions
on our streets, especially in the most hard-hit
areas where people did not return (i.e., the Lower
Ninth Ward and East New Orleans), we saw
many instances of that happening. ARNO
actually has successfully rehabilitated at least ten
dogs that I know of, who have mostly been placed
in homes.*

*As to the conditions on our streets at present . . .
dog rescue still occurs. Most often these days it is
a dog that has had puppies in an abandoned
building or a dog that landed in bad hands . . .
dogfighting or cruelty are the usual suspects. Dogs
are still being turned in by people who cannot
afford to keep them, including Gulf Coast
fishermen and people affected by the BP oil spill.*

I am happy to arrange for you to meet Charlotte Bass Lilly, whom I think you would enjoy meeting. Charlotte is a character; she is so New Orleanian and yet is also very unique. She is the executive director of ARNO and she can tell you harrowing stories of rescue after Katrina. I also have rescue stories; mine involved a lot of reunions since I was a part of Stealth Volunteers (a group formed after Katrina to help rescue and reunite animals that were sent to shelters all over the U.S.). I myself was involved with ten reunions, and our organization was responsible for close to 2,500 animals being reunited with their owners. Let me know your time frame for spending some time at ARNO and I will see if we can't get Charlotte there to meet you. ARNO is an amazing place, totally run by volunteers; they have placed 5,500 animals in permanent homes since Katrina. It's rudimentary in the way it looks; they operate out of a warehouse in

*Harahan (a town nearby New Orleans) and
things are pretty bare-bones there. But the
animals are given vet care and nursed back to
health if they need it, and then are adopted, so it
works, even if it is done on a shoestring.*

I was eager to meet both Laura and Charlotte.
Whenever I told people I did dog rescue, they seemed to
picture me hanging from a cliff with a rope tied around
my waist, pulling a dog to safety. In reality, most of my
rescues involved being handed a leash, sometimes with a
dog bed and a bowl. Laura and Charlotte appeared to
be more of the cape-wearing type.

With some concrete plans lined up, Paul and I
booked our flights and hotel and set off for the first trip
since our honeymoon.

We stayed in a charming hotel in the French Quarter; it was supposedly haunted by the ghosts of dead
authors Tennessee Williams, Ernest Hemingway, and
Truman Capote. As we checked in, there was a man at
a table in the lobby with shoulder-length gray hair.

"Look," I said, "Mark Twain's ghost!" That started us on four days of quietly pointing to every guest in the place: "The ghost of William Styron, the ghost of Erma Bombeck, the ghost of James Patterson." No one was safe from our relentless ghost-hunting.

We arrived on a Wednesday night, very tired and out of sorts, but we had dinner plans with my friend Ken, who, in addition to rescuing pit bulls, writes about dogs. He has a mysterious animal magnetism—well, more like a stray-dog magnetism. I believe he could find a homeless dog at the Lancôme counter in Saks. At home we never went out to dinner. I was a big fan of eating at the same time toddlers and senior citizens ate (five-thirty at the latest) and being in bed before the clock struck double digits. This time, when we took a cab to the restaurant, it was about nine p.m. New York time, and there was a steady downpour. We had no idea where we were. It was absolutely *crazy* of us. We arrived and sat down to dinner with Ken and other friends old and new. We ate a great meal, had wine with dinner, and indulged in dessert—three things that were completely out of character for us; we were this close to getting T-shirts that said I GOT BOURBON FACED ON SHIT STREET.

The next day we woke up late and ate that gloriously stacked breakfast buffet. I went to the workout room at the hotel while Paul read the paper, and then we got dressed for our leisurely day. Friday we'd be spending with Ken visiting the LA/SPCA and some of his rescued dogs and that night we'd be having dinner with Laura and Charlotte from ARNO.

We walked around the French Quarter and kept talking about how great it was to be so at liberty. It was thrilling, in fact! We talked about Violet and our dogs and how funny it was to have a discussion without being interrupted by a needy child or a rambunctious dog. We were drunk with freedom; we'd walk by an art gallery and say, "We can go in here!" (We almost bought a triptych of a Boston terrier, but stopped ourselves when we realized we had a living triptych of Boston terriers at home.) A bit later we wanted to try the beignets we'd been told so much about, so we stepped into a café. We looked at the menu and began to order. They said whatever we got would have to be to go; even though it was two forty-five in the afternoon, they were closing. So we left, but quickly found another café that wasn't closing, and ordered beignets. And they were okay! We gave our assessment of the cakelike item:

"It's kind of crulleresque, don't you think?" I mused.

"Mmm, yes," Paul agreed. "Cruller slash bow tie."

"I imagined it to be more doughnutish."

"Yes, it reminds me of a zeppole."

"It's good, but I'd rather have an apple cider doughnut."

"No question about it," he said. "A fresh cider doughnut beats all."

After the beignet colloquium we wandered around a little more in the Quarter. Pretty much everything was closed, unless we wanted a tour of graveyards.

We had no idea what to do with ourselves, and we'd run through all of our talking points.

"Do we have nothing left to say to each other?" I said.

"That's impossible!" Paul said. "We are two very

interesting people with a lot in common, and we've barely spoken in the last eight years."

The city was uncharacteristically freezing, so we decided to head back to our hotel. We started looking up places to eat dinner and we realized how tired we were from the trip, the walking around, the wine. There was a restaurant in the hotel and we decided to eat in. We were ready for bed by nine o'clock.

It was a little funny (or sad) how much we looked forward to simply having a room without dogs. I walked around with socks on and never once stepped into a surprise puddle. We realized we needed that first day just to come to terms with what we could do, suddenly remembering what it had felt like before we were married and became parents and had so many dogs. It was quiet. And dry.

The next morning we had more of a schedule. Ken was coming to breakfast, and then we were off to see some animals. At breakfast Ken and I talked about what had been going on in New Orleans animal rescue. He explained that there had been a bit of a crisis a month before when the LA/SPCA's contract with New Orleans for animal control did not look like it was going to be renewed.

"I was ready to leave town," Ken said.

They ultimately came to an agreement, and Ken didn't move away. After breakfast we headed to the LA/SPCA in New Orleans. On the way, I asked Ken if he liked this shelter.

"I do," he said. "I approached them with someone else about implementing a program to spend time with dogs who were going to be put down."

He said Bad Rap, the legendary pit bull rescue in Oakland, California (they took in Michael Vick's pit bulls who'd been used in a dogfighting ring), had been successful with this. "Just an opportunity for a dog who has never known love in his life to experience it . . . just once before he or she dies." The shelter had refused, which was disappointing to him. To me it sounded like an extraordinary and very moving idea.

I was used to shelters in New York City, which in general were not cheery places, and some were worse than others. Always when I went to these facilities, though, it was to pick up a specific dog, so that was my focus. I had never been to a shelter and not left with a dog. Walking into the LA/SPCA, Paul and I talked about our need to avoid looking any dog square in the eyes. As soon as we entered the lobby, we saw a woman at the admitting desk dumping the six puppies her unneutered female had had—she had apparently done this before, with this dog's first litter. She looked at me with sad eyes asking if I would like to adopt them, and I just said, "No, thank you." Not two inches from where she sat was a poster advertising low-cost and free spaying and neutering. Her laziness had resulted in the birth of at least twelve unwanted dogs, and I was not sympathetic to her.

A young woman named Kim came out to show us around and we walked to the back with her. The setup was adult dogs first and then puppies (they wanted people to see the less adoptable dogs first). Through no fault of their own, some dogs have a harder time finding homes. I had recently read that black Labs or Lab mixes are euthanized at a much higher rate at pounds and shelters because people pass them up for lighter-colored dogs, which stunned me. I knew that with my own rescue group, the seniors were the last to get picked. I thought the setup here was quite brilliant, since before I got to the puppies, I saw at least ten mature dogs I would've taken if I was looking for one. Having been an owner of puppies (not on purpose), I was a huge advocate for older dogs. Sure, puppies are cute, but they need a ton of attention and training. They bite their leashes and eat their beds; they relieve themselves everywhere. A reporter once asked me if I could show her some of the damage to my home and personal property done by my puppies. I gave her a walking tour of the trail of destruction: chewed armchairs, stained carpets, poor Violet's stuffed animals with missing eyes and dolls with missing hands and feet, a mangled pair of $400 prescription glasses, on and on and on. An adult foster dog would need only a day or two to understand city life housebreaking, and then he would be good to go.

Usually when I went into a shelter I bit down on the insides of my cheeks and tongue. It was a way to keep from crying and look like a supermodel at the same time. Before I learned this trick, I had gone into a couple of shelters and tears sprang from my eyes like I was a cartoon baby. I didn't feel that way here, though. Honestly, the cages the dogs were in were, well, really nice. They were very large, wide and tall and divided into two parts so they could be easily cleaned. The dogs had fine little cots and blankets and bowls, except for one guy who had a sign on his cage that said DON'T GIVE ME TOWELS OR BLANKETS, I WILL EAT THEM! (I was very impressed with his writing skills, as well as his honesty and self-awareness.) I mean, it wasn't home sweet home, but it sure wasn't hell. There were two dogs who were quite emotionally attached to each other, so the shelter staff put them in the same cage. One was sleeping on top of the cot and the other was underneath. Around the corner was the puppy room. Of course they were adorable, but I didn't worry about them; they had not suffered yet and they would be the first to get adopted. I was talking to Ken and looking around, and all of a sudden he was holding this tiny, unbelievably soft little doe-eyed gray puppy.

"Where'd you get that?" I said, surprised.

"What?" Ken said. "I don't know what you're talking about. C'mon, let's go." He pretended to slip the pup into his jacket.

The shelter worker wrestled the puppy away from Ken (not really, but almost) because they were having a big puppy adoption event that weekend and they needed all the puppies they could get.

It was the older dogs who got to me. One sweet black dog jumped up on the cage and tried to lick me through the bars. I scratched behind his ears.

"You are going to find a great home, Newton," I said to him, "because you have lovely soft eyes and a good heart."

Paul looked at me and smiled. He was stuck like glue to the cage of a brown pit mix who had chosen him. The dog kept pawing at him. I knew he'd find a home, too. The ones I worried about were the sad, lost little souls who didn't have the confidence to stride on up to someone and say, "Take me, we'll make it work."

We toured around more and saw some of the areas they'd be turning into outdoor runs. We also met a very mean cat who was shaved except for her giant lion's head. It turned out she was allergic to herself. That would make anyone mean!

After the LA/SPCA, we visited a few of Ken's foster dogs, all pit bulls, who were being housed at a doggie day care. One was a refugee from a Florida dogfighting case, the sweetest fellow, Andy. He had grown close to a pretty dog named Marissa. We took them out to a run so they could play together, and it was just so adorable to see how much they loved each other. Andy jumped up on me and scratched my cheek. It didn't hurt, but a stream of blood started running down my face. I was trying to act nonchalant while resembling a Madonna statue with bloody tears. Inside we met another of Ken's dogs, a beautiful gray female that he found attempting to board a bus on Martin Luther King Day. He named her Rosa Parks.

When we'd kissed the dogs good-bye, we decided to

head back to our hotel and Ken would go home. He needed to pick up one of his dogs from surgery later and we wanted to get cleaned up before dinner with Laura and Charlotte. Ken drove us around the Lower Ninth Ward, where we saw the vast empty spaces that had been filled with houses before Katrina. Many that were abandoned had spray-painted Xs and strange number codes on them.

"What do the Xs mean?" I asked Ken.

"They used those during Katrina," Ken said. "The numbers refer to how many living or dead people were found in the house."

There were other signs painted, like SPCA—TOOK ONE CAT or SPCA—TWO DOGS DEAD. It was nearing six years since the hurricane.

I was telling Paul about Ken's ability to find stray dogs and how I had half expected us to stumble upon one. We were all talking about how glad we were that we hadn't since we were tired and it was cold and getting late.

And then Ken said, "Is that—?"

I looked and saw nothing anywhere.

Paul said, "It looks like a black Lab."

"Rottweiler," Ken said.

Still, I saw nothing. As opposed to having an extra sense like Ken, I seemed particularly senseless. It was true that I also never found Waldo or spotted the hidden picture in those 3-D posters. I was pretty much blind to subtlety.

The area was filled with houses. In fact, we weren't too far from Ken's, so it didn't strike me as likely that what we had seen was a "stray dog," but Ken pulled over and we all got out. I finally saw it as it darted away from us. Ken was driving a rental car because his own was in the shop, so he didn't have any of his "equipment" on hand—the leashes, collars, and treats he kept in his trunk.

"We need food," he said, looking at us.

I took a closer look around; the houses were somewhat ramshackle and we were right beside a train track that ran by the rebuilt levee. I didn't know where we'd get food. I dug through my pockets and found some of my airplane gum and a fuzzy cough drop. I offered them to Ken.

"I'll be back," he told us.

He walked away, and we kept an eye on the black dog. It went up the hill and crossed the tracks; Paul and I followed him. A train was coming, and Paul raced across the track to be on the side of the dog, I stayed so Ken would know where we were (and wouldn't leave us here). He came walking back from somewhere with a coffee cup.

"I've got some chicken," he said. I noticed then that one of the houses was actually a restaurant called Ma's.

"Where's Paul?"

I indicated behind the train. We stood and waited as the cargo train chugged by us. It kept going and going and going. There were empty, open freight cars, the kind that would be perfect if you were going to hop a train. And it wasn't going very fast, so I thought I had a good shot. Where would it go? I guess if I were a hobo, I wouldn't care.

"What if it never ends?" Ken said.

"Well," I said, "I guess we split the chicken."

A few minutes later the last car finally pulled past us. It was some long train, a real show-off.

Ken and I crossed the tracks. There was a strong woody smell, like the boardwalk in Coney Island, and it was windy. Paul sat about ten feet from the dog, who seemed like he wanted to come to him. Ken gave each of us some chicken. I squatted down and spoke in my doggy voice, "Come here, Dr. Pfefferbaum." But he did not respond to our elementary school psychologist's name. "I have some delicious chicken for you! Real chicken! Not by-products." My dogs would've been on my head at this point. But this one couldn't have been less interested.

Ken tried next. "Here, boy," he sang. I was surprised to see he didn't get any further than I did.

Paul plunked himself on a railroad tie and put a piece of chicken a few feet from him. He said nothing. The dog trotted up and ate the chicken.

"What the hell?" I said.

"Obviously," Ken said, "he's not a reader."

Paul did it again, and again the dog came up to him. He was close enough to grab, but then what? Ken called animal control; they recognized his voice. He asked if they could send someone, and they said they would. He hung up and said, "They won't."

I found a piece of rope on the tracks that I attempted to fashion into a leash, though it ended up looking more like an old-time hangman's noose. Something about me absolutely repelled the dog. I was standing there freezing to death and really tired.

"I have to leave," Ken said. "I've got to get my own dog before the vet closes."

"C'mon, you jerk," I said. "Let's go!"

Paul looked at me and raised his eyebrows, and the dog trotted off.

"Let's walk toward the car," Ken said, "maybe he'll follow us."

"Right," I replied, "playing hard-to-get!"

We headed back and passed a construction crew that was working on the waterfront. We asked them if they'd seen the black dog before.

"Oh yeah," the foreman said, "he's around here a lot. Is he yours?"

We said no but that we were trying to get him. Suddenly the construction crew was snapping and clapping and whistling. Their "helping" scared the dog away. He trotted even farther until he was all but a speck. Ken put in calls to some of the rescue groups he worked with around the area, letting them know about the dog.

We circled back again, and this time the dog took off at top speed in the opposite direction. We just weren't going to get him. It was crazy to me; I'd never seen a dog be so unattainable.

We all stood watching, hoping he'd turn around and change his mind, but he didn't. We didn't want to leave him there, but it appeared we'd have no choice.

We got back to the hotel with enough time to wash up and then go to meet Laura, who was picking us up in her yellow Volkswagen Beetle and taking us to Charlotte's, where we'd switch to her station wagon and head out to ARNO.

Charlotte lived in the Garden District, an area

of New Orleans that looked most like the Louisiana of my imagination—filled with historic southern mansions, weeping willows, and an overall feeling of opulence gone by.

We pulled up to a late-nineteenth-century ginger-bread-style "double shotgun" house, an absolutely magnificent example of the neighborhood's architectural splendor. A well-dressed white-haired man walked by us with a cocker spaniel on a leash. The man, it turned out, was Charlotte's husband. In the divide between her house and the one next door, behind a small fence, there were another twelve spaniels, barking their heads off. I thought about what their neighbors must think, and then realized they probably think the same thing that people think when they come to my house and my four dogs go crazy. Four, twelve . . . it was all the same.

We entered through the grand front door and inside I immediately gushed over the Victorian elements: gas-light fixtures, elaborate moldings, intricately carved ceilings and banisters. The equally old wood floors were, well, who knew, because you couldn't find them. Every inch was packed with boxes. The house was actually more filled with crap than my own.

Laura turned to us. "This stuff is all for Barkus. Charlotte runs it." Barkus is the canine version of Mardi Gras, a big parade of costumed dogs and their people. Apparently, a lot of toilet paper was used because there were about a dozen boxes stacked up to the twelve-foot ceilings. There were also birdhouses and dollhouses stuck in various places.

Charlotte came out of the kitchen pulling her hair back. "Hi, y'all, sorry about the mess!" She was younger than I'd pictured her, and very put together, which was a lot more than I could say for myself. We said hello and she disappeared to the back of the house, narrating the chores she was doing along the way.

"Did you say hello to the cat?" she shouted. "Don't!"

Laura pointed to a white fluffy mass. "That's her, that's Ribbons!"

I thought Violet would've loved to meet Ribbons, a white cat with a pretty, girly name.

"Her name is Ribbons because if you try and touch her, she'll cut you to ribbons."

"Oh!" I said, stepping back. "Those kinds of ribbons."

"She's feral," Laura explained, kindly.

Charlotte came back out. "Okay, ready!" She found her keys, purse, cigarettes and lighter, and jacket buried in the maze, and we headed out the door. Her brand-new navy Mercedes-Benz station wagon was parked in front of the house.

"Hang on," she said, looking in. "I gotta clean out some of this junk. There's no place to sit. Let me get a garbage bag."

She disappeared into the house and came out with some Hefty bags. "Here, Laura," she said, handing her one of the bags. "You do the back, I'll do the front."

They opened the doors. The car, which couldn't have been more than a month or so old, was filled in every nook and cranny with papers, fast-food wrappers, and soda cans.

"I'm not sure . . ." Laura said, looking. It was kind of hard to ask someone to decide what was trash in your car. "Hmm," she said, picking up a calendar.

"Throw it out," Charlotte said. "Oh wait, they might want it. You guys want that?"

"That's okay," Paul and I said, watching them, amused. Everything Charlotte picked up she greeted with great interest before designating it trash. "You don't have to clean that much," I said. "We can just shove stuff over."

"Oh, good," Charlotte said. "That's enough then, Laura, they can shove stuff over." She knotted the garbage bags and dropped them on the curb. She spoke in a very gently southern accent, and not the "Yat" dialect that I'd been hearing. (It was called Yat because instead of "How are you?" people say "Where y'at?")

We piled in around the stuff and Charlotte started the car. I felt like I had known her my whole life, this restless, messy, good-hearted person. I loved her. It was about a forty-minute drive to the ARNO shelter in Harahan, Louisiana, and I seized my chance to ask Charlotte some questions while she was unable to move.

"So you were one of the original ARNO people, right?"

She told me about how ARNO came together, started by an out-of-town volunteer (a tan, blond Californian who was referred to as "Rescue Barbie"), and how they needed a local to run things when she left. Charlotte was the obvious choice. She'd been in rescue for a long time and had been in the trenches during Katrina.

She turned to Laura in the passenger seat and said, "Can we please turn this damn heat down, I'm blazing!"

"I'm always cold," Laura said, smiling. "Charlotte's always hot."

She shut the heat off and continued. "We were out there in the boats, you know. We had to have our RESCUE shirts on so they'd let us alone."

Otherwise, the mandatory evacuation would have been enforced. She told us about how the water turned to a black sludge, and incredulously recounted how she'd seen bodies floating and how crazy it all was.

"I remember we were out there and we saw this guy floating, and one of the girls on my team knew him! She went to high school with him! We couldn't just leave him there, so we tied him to a light pole."

There was an almost clinical distance in her voice; it was not unlike someone who'd worked in a MASH unit.

"It was so hot!" Charlotte said, dragging out the words. "We had to wear long pants and these giant rubber wader boots and jackets because you know the stuff that was floating was like poison." She looked in the rearview mirror as if she could see it in there.

"It was disgusting and it stank, but I was just blazing, so I said, 'Screw it,' and I took off the boots and socks and rolled up my pants. I couldn't take the heat worse than the junk. My whole crew did the same thing, and the funny thing is, since then none of us has ever had to shave our legs!" She was chuckling. "It was like Katrina Nair."

Charlotte had been born in Germany in 1951; her dad was in the army. He was Jewish and had grown up in New York and Chicago, and her mother was from New Orleans. After the Korean War ended, they moved back to the States. "My father said he wanted to live someplace that didn't snow. He hated the cold, so they moved to New Orleans. So I'm Jewish, too!" she said, looking at me.

Paul looked at me and smiled. I knew what he was thinking. She reminded me of my aunt Mattie and Paul's Italian aunts. They would've been cast in western movies as "saloonkeepers with hearts of gold."

She continued telling us about taking animals to the Lamar-Dixon staging area, where hundreds and hundreds of stranded and abandoned Katrina pets were kept before being transported to shelters around the country.

"Those army guys liked me, because of my dad, you know," she said. "There was one night, we had rescued about forty dogs—they were in crates and it was getting dark, so we had to stay overnight on the roof of this house." She smiled. "The girls had found vodka in there and they brought it up and I was like, 'No way—I'm thirsty enough without getting drunk! That's a bad idea, but you go ahead.' So then the army wanted to send a helicopter to get us out of there! I said, 'Where are you going to land? I've got forty crates tied to the roof of this house, you're going to blow them all into the water!'" She shook her head. "I said, 'No way, forget it, we're fine here.' So we stayed the night. And sure enough, in the morning those girls felt like hell! I knew they shouldn't have drunk all that vodka!"

She turned off on an exit and we drove for about ten minutes. I checked my BlackBerry and there was an e-mail from my friend Judith. She was writing a piece for a beauty magazine on hair removal and was looking for interesting stories. I decided against submitting "Katrina Nair."

"Home sweet home!" Charlotte said, pulling into the driveway of an industrial-looking warehouse, one of many on the street. This was Animal Rescue of New Orleans. It was a prefab office attached to a sort of giant garage with the front open. Floodlights hung from the roof. There was an unceasing bark that rose and fell in volume coming from the building. Charlotte charged in, eager to get in the mix. We walked into the administrative area and I began coughing madly.

"You allergic?" Charlotte asked. "Or is it the stink?"

"It's okay," I said through chokes. "I'm fine."

The smell was pretty putrid; I wasn't exactly sure why. There was a family adopting a dog, and a worker holding a Pomeranian with one eye (his name was One-Eyed Jack), and no one else seemed to be bothered by the smell. It might have been worsened by the fact that I'd just heard about all of the horrid smells during the hurricane.

Charlotte took us to the area where most of the dogs were kept, and it smelled quite nice! I looked around at the large crates and cages. All of the dogs had blankets and towels and were clearly well loved while waiting for adoption. This place was fully staffed with volunteers, as opposed to the LA/SPCA's paid employees—all doing the dirty work at eight o'clock at night with no sign of leaving. A section of the shelter was devoted to feral animals; they worked to get them to a place where they could actually be with a family. It was, in short, breathtaking.

There was another black dog here that I fell in love with. She'd been pregnant and had puppies. I sat down and talked to her and told her how very beautiful she was.

Charlotte walked around and greeted her crew with enthusiasm and mountains of praise. "Wow, did you clean this up? You are a superstar!" I saw how much her staff wanted to please her, and I totally got it, because I did, too.

We went to get in her car to leave and go find someplace for dinner. One of the other ARNO brass, Lise, a younger woman with dark hair, followed us outside. Charlotte introduced us and explained that Lise was their feral expert. She was briefing Charlotte about a situation, and I listened.

"We have volunteers arriving here at nine-thirty and at St. John's Parish at quarter to ten." They were discussing some directions and details that were hard to decipher.

"All right, see you in the morning!" Charlotte said.

We began heading to a restaurant that Laura found.

"What was that about?" I asked.

"Oh, man!" Charlotte exclaimed. "We got a call that there's a dog in St. John's Parish—"

Laura looked back and mouthed, "Really bad area. People have guns at night."

"So the dog's got a pickle jar stuck on his head."

"Huh?" I said.

"It's been on there for five days! Animal control can't get him, and today the LA/SPCA was there for four hours with three people and they couldn't get him." She turned to Laura. "You know he came out five minutes after they left."

She shook her head. "These stupid town people haven't caught him because they're afraid he'll bite them! I'm like, 'He's got a freakin' jar stuck on his head, he can't bite you!' And he's gotta be really weak. Five days with no food and the only water is the condensation from the inside of the jar."

"Oh my God!" I said for about the fiftieth time in the last hour.

"So tomorrow we're getting a posse together because the only way we're going to be able to snag him is if we corner him. Then we'll take him to the vet and sedate him, get the jar off, and we'll take him to ARNO."

Charlotte had made this plan and was on it. The idea of this dog, however, was haunting me, and Paul, too. We were both frowning as we pulled into the restaurant.

It was a complete hole-in-the-wall with the best food I'd ever eaten. While we were waiting (an hour) to get a table, a woman came up to Charlotte. She recognized her from being on the news during a recent cold snap when the shelter needed donations for heating oil. Charlotte was charming and gracious. It was nearing nine o'clock when she mentioned that she hadn't eaten yet today and had been up since three a.m. Suddenly I was starving and could barely stand up. If she wasn't going to act hungry and tired, by gum I'd do it for her.

After dinner she drove us back to our hotel. She was so warm and wonderful I hated to say good-bye.

We went into the hotel and both collapsed. I didn't remember ever feeling this tired, except perhaps when I'd given birth. As the revelers outside our window were just heating up, we conked out.

I woke up at six a.m. and started thinking about this dog Charlotte had called "Jarhead." I felt a clamp on my heart when I thought about him running out there frightened and probably going crazy. Paul woke up and looked at my alarmed expression.

"What's wrong?"

"I'm thinking about Jarhead," I said.

He nodded.

"I think I want to go help them."

"Okay," he said, and headed to the bathroom. I got on my computer and looked at ARNO's Facebook page. There were some posts about Jarhead and the impending rescue with times and addresses. A lot of people commented that they wouldn't be able to come, but they were sending good thoughts. I also noticed on Ken's Facebook feed that the Rottweiler had been picked up by another group, "Dogs of the Ninth Ward." He was now safely deposited at Ken's house and would be going to his vet later that day.

I started looking at how we could get to ARNO to meet up with everyone. I had a fund-raiser to attend at three o'clock and I wasn't sure how long this venture would take. Paul suggested renting a car and that seemed to make the most sense. We were still really tired, and it was our second-to-last day in New Orleans, but we were definitely going to do this.

I didn't really know what I was in for, but I decided to forgo a shower, but not breakfast! We ate well before heading out.

When we drove up to ARNO, we saw Charlotte and two other people talking. She saw us get out of the car, and her face exploded into a grin and she applauded.

"Backup forces," Paul said.

She came over and hugged us both, and Lise came out to address the crowd.

"Okay!" she announced. "First off, the woman from St. John's Parish called to say it is a *may-o-nnaise* jar, not a *pickle* jar! So the situation has been downgraded." She rolled her eyes and we laughed.

"When we get to St. John's, I will give everyone a map, a flashlight, a whistle." She looked around at her audience. "These are not parting gifts—please give them back when we are finished, or you have to leave."

I tried not to think about what the flashlights were for on this bright, sunny morning.

We all drove caravan-style to LaPlace, Louisiana. It looked very familiar, and it turned out the movie *Monster's Ball* had been filmed around here. The meeting point was the St. John Parish Animal Shelter. When we arrived there were about six other people milling about; all together there were about fifteen of us. Of the group, at least three were starting their own shelters; I was impressed with the magnitude of grassroots effort. There was a per-vasive belief here that if something needed to be done, you didn't wait for someone else to do it. The feeling that each person could make a difference was profound.

The animal control officer was a guy named Jerry. He was slight and reminded me of a teacher of mine from elementary school, with the same glasses, mustache, and pale blue windbreaker. He divided us up into groups and explained the plan. Basically, a group would be positioned at every side of Jarhead and if anyone saw him they were supposed to blow the whistle. One of the volunteers raised her hand and asked what the dog looked like.

"He's a dog with a jar on his head!" Lise said. "Please remember, people, that this is a *feral* dog who is most likely going absolutely bonkers at this point."

The people had stopped listening and were playing with their flashlights, which were new, so you had to pull this little piece of paper out from in front of the battery to make them work. The whistles were standard, the maps were clear except we had no idea where we were. They might has well have been maps of the moon.

Charlotte told Paul and me to go with Jerry. I was secretly pleased because it seemed like Jerry would be the one to get him—he had the tranquilizer gun.

Paul and I got in his SUV. He turned the car on and the radio began playing Loggins and Messina's "Thinking of You," just in case Jerry's familiar appearance didn't make me feel enough like it was 1974.

"I'm going to lay the gun like this," he said, positioning the rifle by the passenger seat. "You need to keep the tip pointed up."

He pulled out, the Vanillaroma tree swinging from his rearview mirror. "I can't take the animal control van, because he knows it's me and he'll run," he explained, "so I'm taking this car. Hopefully, today, we'll catch him off-guard."

He started telling us about the past week's frustration trying to get this dog. Jerry had "darted" him once but the dart just bounced off—he was so lean from not eating, there was no fat for it to sink into. Jerry was a kindhearted guy. You could see he was not the Dog Catcher even though technically he was.

We pulled up a street filled with trailer homes on cinder blocks. "I've seen him under the blue house there, and the gray one," Jerry said.

We got out of the car and there were a few of the others around. As my door slammed I heard a whistle, and there he was.

He was small and yellow and there was a jar on his head. He looked like a little space man.

"THERE HE IS!" several people yelled and raced and the whole bit of direction about not frightening him away went out the window. Since everyone else was running, I ran, too. The dog was a puppy, probably four months old. I couldn't believe how quickly we saw him and how tiny he was. The narrative that had been bandied about was that he'd stuck his head in the jar looking for food and got his head caught. It didn't quite make sense to me, only because mayonnaise isn't one of the more delicious foods, but I guess starving dogs felt differently.

The group dispersed and I found myself in the lead. I'm very athletic in a gym. I can run ten miles and row and stairclimb and everything else, but I preferred climate control and my iPod. So here I was running the fastest and the longest, but I wasn't really sure what I'd do when I got to him, because I was outrunning my team with the leash and collar. Fortunately, I had to slow down, as the dog pulled a fast one on me. There was a copse of deadish-looking trees and heavy brambles and thicket. There was no "opening," no neat trail, and so I just forged in, slowly, because prickers were everywhere, catching on my jeans and jacket and brushing my face and snagging my hair. I could see Jarhead about ten feet ahead of me. He was in no rush; he'd gotten through this mess easily, since he had the protective headgear. I was cursing silently as Jerry caught up. I thought he'd have some technique, or a machete, but he wasn't any more clued in about what to do than I was. When I finally got myself into a small clearing, I stepped into a swamp. My heart was going after the dog, but my head was thinking, *These are the only shoes I brought except for flip-flops, these are the only jeans I brought, and I have only one more pair of clean socks.* Would I wear dirty, wet clothes for two days to save a dog? Definitely. Was I looking forward to it? Nope.

Jerry kept falling behind me, and I suddenly realized the movie the area brought to mind was not *Monster's Ball* but *The Blair Witch Project*, the only movie that had ever really scared me. The night after we watched it, I was walking my dog on the grassy median between Upper and Lower Riverside Drive, essentially twenty feet of lawn and a few trees, and I started to panic. When I came back into my apartment, Paul had tied Q-tips up with dental floss into a little Blair Witch pile and left it in the bathroom. The movie had made me feel like New York's Riverside Park was too rural. Which begs the question, would I get captured by the Blair Witch to save a dog?

"You know, when you're crouching down," Jerry called out to me, "your blond hair looks like the dog. Maybe don't do that. I don't want to shoot you in the behind."

I looked at him incredulously.

"It won't kill you or nothing," he said, comforting me, "but you'll sleep a good long while."

Oh good, because I definitely wanted to sleep in this

swampy, brambly marsh near the people who came out at night with guns.

"I will try my best not to crouch, Jerry."

The next area we hit was a stream. The little yellow dog had gone through the stream, and even though my shoes were wet already, they could still be called simply damp. But if I went in the stream they'd be soaked, no question about it. I walked quickly and found a small cluster of rocks that I could leap onto and get out without getting too much wetter. I was also sweating a lot. I did not feel nice at all.

Jerry followed me through.

"Dog rescue in Manhattan is a little different," I said.

He chuckled. "You don't really have swamps there, do you?"

"No, but we have the Boat Pond in Central Park."

Throughout this we were hearing various whistles blown. Jarhead was being sighted all around and thus far the whole cornering him thing was not working, as he who hadn't eaten in days and had a jar on his head was still outrunning and outsmarting us all.

I lost Jerry again and called Paul on his cell phone. He was somewhere in someone's yard and his sneakers were wet. "Mine too!" I said. "And my socks!" I was just grateful it hadn't been worse, like a nail breaking.

I found myself in a field and Jarhead was at the other end. I started running, trying very hard not to crouch, all the while keeping my eyes on Jarhead. I moved in on him as he ran up a hill. There was a train on a track and he easily went under it. I stopped and looked around me, and there was no one. I thought, *Will I dive under a train to save a dog?* And then I held my breath and went under and made it out the other side. Jarhead was racing up the train tracks and I was running behind him. Suddenly some of the others were there, which was a relief since the thought occurred to me that I had no idea where in the heck I was other than somewhere in Louisiana.

The only way to keep up with Jarhead was to run on the railroad ties. Between them were big rocks, and hopping on them was sort of like, but worse than, running on the beach.

Another guy and I were closing in on Jarhead, but just like that he turned off the tracks and into a ravine and was gone again. We stopped running and looked around. The guy took out a cigarette and lit up. Just then we heard the whistle and a lot of shouting. I heard someone yell, "She got 'im!"

We high-fived and walked around the train tracks to a back road and headed toward the shelter. One of the other volunteers, a guy in a white van with a giant cartoon dog painted on it, pulled over and offered us a ride.

"So they got him?" I said.

"They got him and lost him again," he said. A couple had caught him, slipped a leash over his head, and taken off the jar. The dog proceeded to bite the woman six times, she dropped the leash, and he was gone again.

Charlotte was in the parking lot with Lise and some of the others, smiling. They heard he had been caught; they hadn't heard he'd been lost again.

"Shoot! Why the heck'd she take off the jar!" Charlotte said. "What'd she think he'd do? He's completely out of his mind!"

Just then Paul and some others walked up. The story was repeated several times. She got him on the leash, took off the jar, he bit her six times. Why the heck did she take the jar off him?

Someone came out of the shelter and told us the woman had gone to the emergency room.

"What?" Lise was flabbergasted. "Because she got bit? Is she going to get her hand amputated?"

I understood what Lise was talking about; there was a need to defend Jarhead lest anyone think he was dangerous. I also felt sorry for the woman who'd gotten bit. In my experience the physical pain of a dog bite was almost secondary to the way it hurt my feelings (*"I'm on your side!"*). Of course, I've been bitten about half a million times now.

Paul and I were off to the side watching.

"Well, we can forget getting him for today," Charlotte said, disappointed.

"That's for sure."

At least he would be able to breathe and eat and drink. Having scoured the area so vigilantly, I had taken note of the amount of fresh water available.

Jerry said he'd put out humane traps later. (Dog traps were just like the little Havahart mouse traps we used when I was growing up, except big enough for a dog.) And we all dispersed, hugging Charlotte good-bye for the second time.

Paul and I got in the car and talked about our separate experiences. We hadn't been able to stay together through most of it.

"It was really kind of amazing," I said. "When I saw him, it was like, 'Hey, that is a dog with a jar on its head.'"

"My favorite part," Paul responded, "was at the end when everyone turned on the woman who'd gotten bitten."

That made me laugh.

"They wanted to make it very clear," I said, "that it was her fault, not Jarhead's."

"Clearly she provoked him!" Paul responded.

"My favorite part," I said, "was how you and I were the only ones complaining about getting wet and muddy."

"It was very wet!" Paul said with mock outrage. "And we're not from around here!"

I looked down at my jeans; the prickers had snagged dozens of nubs, like I had been attacked by very short wolves. I rolled up my jeans and my legs were covered in scrapes.

"I want to go to the emergency room, too," I said, "for severe scrapiotomies."

"You better not. The Women of ARNO will go after you!"

We went back to the hotel and showered and put on fresh clothes for the benefit. I felt I had been changed by this experience. Paul was sitting on the bed and I wanted to share my feelings with him.

"You know," I told him, "I feel like I discovered something about myself today."

He nodded patiently.

"I realized that I am the kind of person who would dive under a train to save a dog."

He smiled at me. "You know that train wasn't connected to an engine," he said.

"What the hell does that mean?" I said, pretty sure he was pulling on my Superman cape.

"Well," he said gently, "it means that the train couldn't move."

"So what?" I said defensively. "It wasn't dangerous?"

"Not really."

"Oh yeah?" I said. "It was windy today. It could've blown over on me."

"That's true."

"And crushed me."

"Yep."

"This is a town known for its hurricanes."

"I'd forgotten that," he admitted.

"I could have been pancaked."

All right, so maybe I hadn't been in that much danger, and maybe I was really more suited for the kind of rescue where dogs trot into your home wearing cable-knit sweaters. Before we'd come to New Orleans, I'd read Dave Eggers's remarkable book *Zeitoun*, which tells the story of one family during Katrina, and the father who stays behind during the evacuation to help. I questioned myself repeatedly when I read it: "Could I do that?" I guess all people have their things. Even brave Indiana Jones can't bear snakes (I can't either). My worst fear, though, was being abandoned somewhere. It has always been what's rooted me to New York City—the fact that you don't have to worry about getting left behind, there is always a cab or a train or a bus to get you home. There aren't woods to get lost in or remote truck stops. It felt to me like help was always a whistle away.

When Jerry and I were slogging through the swamp in search of Jarhead, I was blathering on about how daunted I was by this type of rescue. We were in the backcountry with no idea what we'd find.

"We got McDonald's," he observed, "and Shoney's."

All right, so maybe it wasn't the Amazon rainforest.

"What about you?" he asked. "You could not pay me enough money to walk around New York City!"

"Really?" I said. He began his description of New York City as an urban Wild West with piles of garbage dumped around. "What about Bloomingdale's?" I said.

In the end we were each comfortable in our own habitat. I wasn't afraid to go into a shelter in Harlem or East New York, and he would do whatever it took to get a dog out of the dangers of St. John's Parish. It was in fact his job. He went on to tell me a story of a dog that rescued a blind cat during the hurricane, and another dog that barked until someone came to rescue his elderly owner. So many stories of heroic dogs. I had my own store of them. And that really was the point. I had always felt that any dog I took care of would've done the same for me if it could, and in fact by rescuing them they filled my heart in such a way that I was rescued right back.

I told people at the benefit the incredible story of the attempted rescue of Jarhead. Ken was there and he announced that he was naming "our" Rottweiler Paul Leo, after my husband, who was right proud.

The next day it was time to return home and rescue my mother, who was with Violet and my four dogs, at least two of which had diarrhea. "Why do they always run to have it on carpeting?" she asked me on the phone, defeated.

I spent my first day back shampooing our rugs and thinking about Paul Leo the Rottweiler and Jarhead.

Ken e-mailed me photos with captions like "Paul Leo Rottweiler likes belly rubs!" And I'd reply, "So does Paul Leo human!" We were bummed but not surprised to hear that Paul Leo Rottweiler had tested positive for heartworm, but was about to begin treatment. (Mercifully, Paul Leo human did not have heartworm.)

I also closely monitored the story of Jarhead. Jerry had gotten near enough to take some lovely pictures and it turned out Jarhead was a girl. He also said that after looking at her photos, he was certain that she was the last surviving puppy of a litter he had pulled from the area about four months before. All of the puppies died at the shelter from illness, and Jerry went back to the spot he found them originally, because he was sure that he had left puppies behind. When he went back, he found one dead puppy. That meant that this dog was the only one to survive that litter and had taken pretty good care of herself, until the jar incident. Also, Jerry had taken to calling her the less offensive "Pickles."

A few days after we got home, Pickles was finally caught in the dog trap. Soon after, Jerry was approached by a woman from the street where Pickles had been found. She told him that Pickles had not gotten her head stuck in that jar while trying to get food. The woman had actually seen some kids grab the little yellow dog and jam the jar on her head.

More often than not, what animals require our protection from is not hurricanes or fires, but abuse at the hands of other people.

Pickles, aka Jarhead, was renamed again because ARNO had another dog in the shelter who was already called Pickles. They decided that since there was no label on the jar, it could easily have been a jar of jalapeño peppers, so they named their new girl Pepper.

I spoke to Lise from ARNO, who was overseeing Pepper's rehabilitation and socialization.

"Well, sometimes you get what you asked for," she

laughed, "and she is a little Pepper!" Lise also said that Pepper was making faster progress than most ferals.

"We keep her in a run where although we don't walk her yet, she watches us come and go with other dogs. She is very vocal with us, telling us off all the time, and wagging her tail as she does it!" She continued, "Sometimes she runs under her bed and we just pick it up and pet her, which we can tell makes her very mad, but very happy at the same time." She paused. "Damn, that kind of thing feels good."

After nearly two months, Lise felt it was almost time—about another two to four weeks—for Pepper to be leash trained. And then? Well, once you can walk on a leash, anything is possible. You can be part of a family, participate in society, stroll among your peers.

It was a wonderful feeling to have shared in the rescue of Pepper. Part of me was proud just for having participated in something so far out of my comfort zone. It wasn't something that I felt I'd need to do again, though. I'm happy to remain an urban rescuer.

For their part, the dogs of New Orleans were well

taken care of by remarkably caring people who didn't stop in their tracks for a pricker bush.

Charlotte and I kept in touch about our various rescues. She told me the news that Lise's dog, Boy, had passed on. He was the very definition of a rescue dog, having taken two years to track and trap post-Katrina. Stealth volunteers had searched more than a year for his owners, but never found them. After that he lived with Lise (though he was considered a "red zone," or dangerous and vicious, dog), and they adored each other.

Lise eulogized Boy:

This morning, at 4:56 a.m., I had the honor of feeling his last breath on my face and feeling the last beat of his heart pulse into my hand as I hugged him and sent him on his final journey. Boy, you have been my cherished friend for three years and although I would love to have made you mine sooner, that two years you outran, outsmarted, and challenged me is something I wouldn't trade for anything. You taught me, more

than anyone or anything else in this world, how
not to ever give up.

As evidenced by her work with Pepper, she wasn't giving up.

So we all gave what we could where we were most needed. We were all pursuing the same goals in our own territory, to make the lives of some unfortunate dogs a little better. And the experiences with the dogs changed us, too. If there was something I couldn't do myself, I knew I was a part of this global community, with friends who would be able to help me. We found ourselves more committed and tenacious and resolved and confident. And empathic.

I've discovered that I can pretty much do anything, or at the very least try, without giving up.

Rescuers don't have capes and wrist web-shooters and X-ray vision, but there is a superpower that comes from knowing you're making a difference in the world around you. And like the ability to walk on a leash, it makes anything feel possible.

In loving memory of Clementine Eve Bows

Acknowledgments

I want to thank Esther Newberg, who, daily, makes me feel like the luckiest writer in the world. She's as remarkable a friend as she is an agent, and she's the best agent. Also, she's mean to people who deserve it.

I am eternally grateful to Geoff Kloske for taking me under his oversized, fleece-covered wing and teaching me life lessons on humility, compassion, grace, and sales figures.

There were a lot of ups and a lot of downs writing this book, and Megan Lynch was always there for me. I can never thank her enough for her kindness, brilliance, insight, and sensitivity, and for always making me look tan.

Huge bouquets to all my book fairies: Mih-Ho Cha, Marilyn Ducksworth, Kate Stark, Kari Stuart, Lyle Morgan, Victoria Comella, Lydia Hirt, Ali Cardia, Keely Hild, Gina Rizzo, the Riverhead sales force, and Susan Petersen Kennedy.

Thunderous applause to my beloved Hash Hags, Ann Lembeck Leary and Laura Faye Zigman.

And thanks to friends, teachers, rescuers, and all-around angels and honey buns Barbara Warnke, Jancee Dunn, Judith Fiorillo Newman, Kristin Moavenian, Amy Harmon, Patty Marx, Denis Leary, Susan Orlean, Tim Hutton, Claudia Glaser Mussen, Wendy Hammond, Brenda Copeland, Lauren Gilbert, Tammy Wilson, John Searles, Martha Broderick, Nancy Goldstein, Abby Esselin, Sheryl Trent, Joy Riley, Carolyn McCarthy, Leslie Verbitsky, Vesna Jovanovic, Jodi Groff, Melissa A.

ACKNOWLEDGMENTS

Kaufman, Rose Navales, A. N. Devers, Heather Brausa, Vick Mickunas, Karen Dalton-Beninato, John Sellers, Charlotte Bass Lilly, Laura Bergerol, Ken Foster, Veronica Brooks-Sigler, and Lise McComiskey.

A big chunk of my heart goes to the sweetest, dearest friend, Nicole Leibman, who also happens to be the best vet in the whole universe.

And love to my family, especially those who suffered at the paws of my unhousebroken dogs, especially Violet and Paul.

All right, enough already! xoxox

Learn More About the Rescue Groups

Animal Rescue New Orleans

http://www.animalrescueneworleans.org

Dogs of the 9th Ward

http://dogsofthe9thward.blogspot.com

Northeast Boston Terrier Rescue

http://www.nebostonrescue.org

The Simon Foundation

http://www.thesimonfoundation.org

Sula Foundation

www.sulafoundation.com